WORKBOOK

COMPUTER CONFIDENCE:
A CHALLENGE FOR TODAY

2D EDITION

JAMES F. CLARK, Ph.D.
Clark Systems Corporation

BEVERLY OSWALT, Ed.D.
University of Central Arkansas

DL01BD
PUBLISHED BY
SOUTH-WESTERN PUBLISHING CO.
CINCINNATI, OH   DALLAS, TX   LIVERMORE, CA

Copyright © 1991

by SOUTH-WESTERN PUBLISHING CO.
Cincinnati, Ohio

ALL RIGHTS RESERVED

The text of this publication, or any part thereof, may not be reproduced or transmitted in any form or by any means, electronic or mechanical, including photocopying, recording, storage in an information retrieval system, or otherwise, without the prior written permission of the publisher.

ISBN: 0-538-60185-X

4 5 6 7 8 9 DH 9 8 7 6 5 4

Printed in the United States of America

Apple Computer, Inc. makes no warranties, either express or implied, regarding the enclosed computer software package, its merchantability, or its fitness for any particular purpose. The exclusion of implied warranties is not permitted by some states. The above exclusion may not apply to you. This warranty provides you with specific legal rights. There may be other rights that you may have which vary from state to state.

PREFACE

This workbook is designed to be used with *COMPUTER CONFIDENCE: A Challenge for Today* by Clark and Oswalt. The study guides and exercises in this workbook are designed to supplement the textbook and reinforce the concepts presented in the textbook.

This workbook contains questions and activities for each chapter in the textbook. Completion questions are available for each chapter. In addition, other activities, such as crossword puzzles, word searches, matching exercises, and identification questions, are available for each chapter. Beginning with Chapter 3, "Working at the Computer" activities are included for each chapter. These activities encourage the hands-on use of the computer.

A template disk is available to support the activities in the "Working at the Computer" sections of the chapters. The template disk contains data files for use with many of the computer activities. The use of these files makes practice on the computer more efficient by reducing the amount of keyboarding time required for each activity. The template disk is available for use with the following software packages:

1. PFS:First Choice® [1] (IBM® PC, PC/XT®, and Personal System/2®;[2] and Tandy® [3] 1000)
2. AppleWorks® [4] (Apple® IIe, IIc, and IIGS® [5])
3. MicroTools™:[6] Integrated Software for Word Processing, Spreadsheet, and Database (IBM PC, PC/XT, and Personal System/2; Tandy 1000; and Apple IIe, IIc, and IIGS)

Before completing the exercises in the workbook, read the corresponding chapter in the text. Your teacher will provide you with instructions concerning the use of the workbook and the template disk.

---

[1] PFS:First Choice is a registered trademark of Software Publishing Corporation.

[2] IBM, PC/XT, and Personal System/2 are registered trademarks of International Business Machines Corporation.

[3] Tandy is a registered trademark of Tandy Corporation.

[4] AppleWorks is a registered trademark licensed to CLARIS Corporation by Apple Computer, Inc.

[5] Apple and IIGS are registered trademarks of Apple Computer, Inc.

[6] MicroTools is a trademark of South-Western Publishing Company.

CONTENTS

CHAPTER 1	Computers, Society, and You	1
CHAPTER 2	The Computer System	7
CHAPTER 3	Word Processing Software	13
CHAPTER 4	Spreadsheet Software	23
CHAPTER 5	Database Software	33
CHAPTER 6	Computer Graphics and Graphs	41
CHAPTER 7	Computer Communication	51
CHAPTER 8	Software Integration	61
CHAPTER 9	System Software	67
CHAPTER 10	Input Devices and Media	73
CHAPTER 11	Output Devices and Media	81
CHAPTER 12	Storage Devices and Media	89
CHAPTER 13	Introduction to Programming	97
CHAPTER 14	Logo	107
CHAPTER 15	Programming in BASIC	115
CHAPTER 16	Computers, Careers, and You	125
APPENDIX A	Start-up Procedures	133

Name _____ Class _____ Date _____

CHAPTER 1

Computers, Society, and You

COMPLETION QUESTIONS

1. The _____ may be the most important invention affecting your life.
2. The importance of the computer can be compared to the discovery of the _____, _____, or _____.
3. Computers are advertised on _____, in _____, and in _____.
4. _____ use computers to help keep track of the large amount of money that they receive and give out every day.
5. When someone uses an automatic teller machine to withdraw, deposit, or transfer funds the process is called _____.
6. A _____ society would mean that we would live during a time when cash would not be needed and all money would be transferred electronically from one bank to another.
7. The _____ is a series of bars that represents information.
8. A _____ terminal is used to keep track of every item sold and to deduct the item from the inventory.
9. _____ is a two-way electronic information service that allows the user to view products, select, and purchase products from home.

10. Smart houses use computers to control _____, _____, _____, and _____.

11. _____ programs can be used to teach English, math, history, science, and many other subjects.

12. The shows and movies that you see on television are scheduled by the use of a _____.

13. Computers are used to add _____ to old black-and-white films.

14. _____ are connected to computers to blend sounds and make quality recordings.

15. Computers are used to predict the weather and keep track of _____ and _____.

16. Computers are used in all areas of _____ to keep track of railroad cars, to keep planes from running into each other, and to drive subway and commuter trains.

17. Computerized _____ can pinpoint a location on a map when a call for help comes in to the fire or police station.

18. Computers are used in sports to _____ for teams, _____ statistics, and _____ for events like the Olympics.

19. The travel industry is able to process thousands of reservations for _____, _____, _____, _____, and other related services.

20. Whole body _____ are possible through a scanner that is hooked to the computer.

21. Computers are used to control _____ arms and legs that are used by people who have lost their own arms and legs.

22. A _____ allows people to hold a conference where they can see each other on television monitors and talk to each other by using the telephone.

23. Through _____ people can choose to work at home by using a computer hooked to a telephone.

24. _____ are being used in industry to make cars and other products.

25. Computers are used to help design products like cars by using a computer program called a _____ program.

Name _____ Class _____ Date _____

MATCHING EXERCISES

Match the following terms with their uses. Write the letter of each term on the appropriate line.

- A. bill-payment-by-phone services
- B. universal product code
- C. computer-aided design
- D. robots
- E. videotex
- F. telecommuting
- G. teleconference

1. _____ grocery store
2. _____ computerized banking
3. _____ used to design cars
4. _____ working at home
5. _____ shopping at home
6. _____ meeting with people in another city
7. _____ used to run forklifts

WHAT AM I?

Fill in the terms that best match the clues given.

1. I am a series of bars printed on items in the grocery stores. What am I?

   _____

2. I am a computer program that engineers use to design products. They use me to draw an object on a screen and change its dimensions to get the right design. What am I?

   _____

3. I am a computer program that helps students learn subjects like English and math. What am I?

   _____

4. I am the process that allows people to electronically withdraw, deposit, and transfer money by using automatic teller machines. What am I?

   _____

5. I am the process that allows people to see products on their television screens and buy them using a computer and a telephone. What am I?

   _____

Chapter 1 ♦ Computers, Society, and You

6. I am a computerized cash register that keeps a record of items sold and updates inventory. What am I?

   _____

7. I am the process of working at home and sending work to the office by using a computer hooked to a telephone. What am I?

   _____

8. I am used to help business people hold a conference and talk to each other even when they are in different cities. What am I?

   _____

Name _____ Class _____ Date _____

CROSSWORD PUZZLE

Complete the following Crossword Puzzle. All answers to the puzzle can be found in Chapter 1 of your textbook.

Across Clues
1. universal product code
5. working at home
7. computer-assisted instruction
8. reads UPC on products
9. used in place of exploratory surgery
11. society where all money is transferred electronically

Down Clues
2. computer-aided design
3. terminal that keeps track of inventory
4. shopping at home
5. conference between cities
6. electronic funds transfer
10. performs dangerous or boring tasks for humans

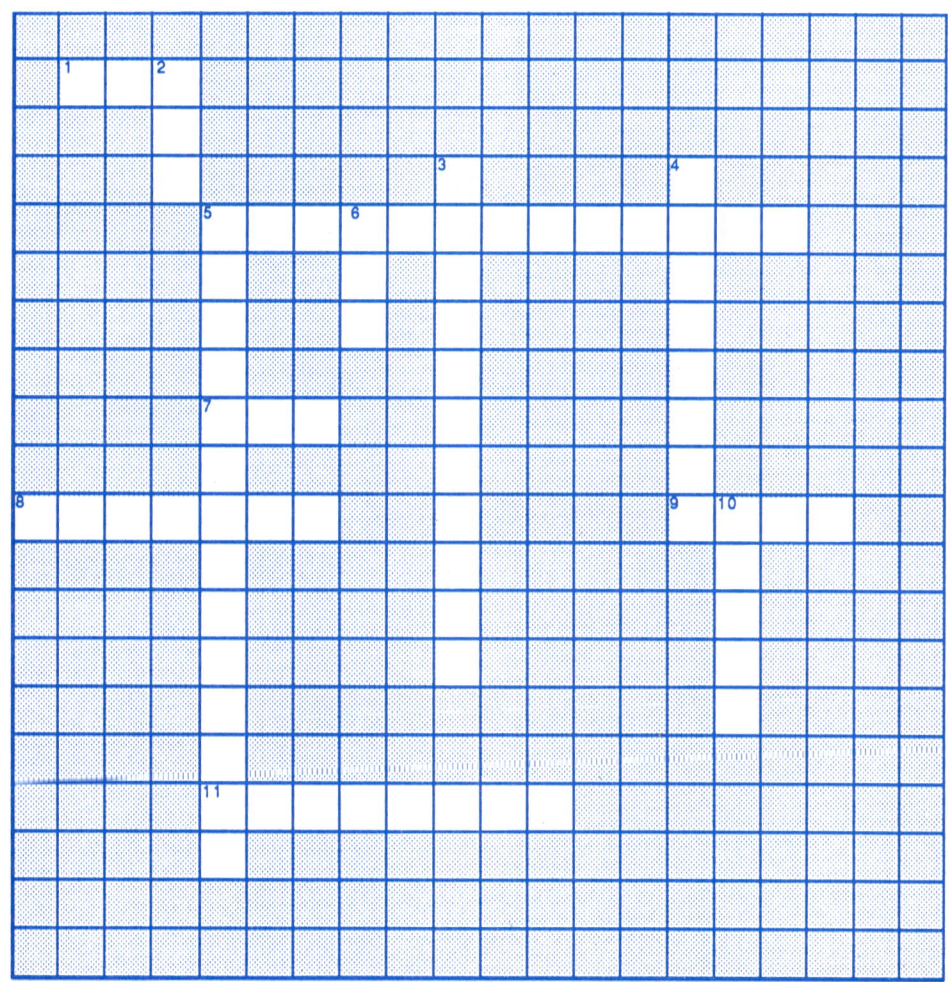

Chapter 1 ♦ Computers, Society, and You

WORD SEARCH

From the scrambled letters below, find and circle the terms that match the following definitions. The terms may be read in any direction and at any angle.

1. shopping at home
2. abbreviation for computer program that teaches English and other subjects
3. working at home using a computer
4. abbreviation for computer program that helps a user design products
5. holding a conference with workers in another city
6. abbreviation for process of depositing, withdrawing, or transferring money electronically
7. abbreviation for bar-code numbers found on most products

```
Y R M R D O C H B F L D L G B G B C
C I R W C I A C V T L N C S E O M T
W Q P J E H Q F O Q A F E F T K W E
Y D D W A Y D S U U L G P A S Q Y L
P P S Y C C Z F P Q C H U V F V A E
K R R W M A G H C Z F I P I L S E C
L K L M X G D W A F D P H D L G H O
O U P X X G P R O S W P Q E P W Y M
M J B P A L W H A R T L E O Y U P M
O I I P X T U I P L J G A T I E K U
K A I C X P E F O M E C M E T A U T
C E C W Y E V W E P S P Y X Q C B I
A G G T G W L X U Y B A R Z D P G N
F Q T E L E C O N F E R E N C E O G
W P Z S B G T T H Q C V N E Y Z E M
```

6   Workbook ♦ *Computer Confidence: A Challenge for Today*

Name _____ Class _____ Date _____

CHAPTER 2

The Computer System

COMPLETION QUESTIONS

1. A computer system processes facts known as _____.
2. The visible, touchable parts of a computer are known as the _____.
3. The invisible, electronically stored instructions that tell a computer what to do are known as _____.
4. A group of devices and procedures for performing a task is known as a _____.
5. An information system is a system that processes _____.
6. The data that enters a system is known as _____.
7. Useful information that leaves a system is known as _____.
8. The steps that make sure everything that should be done to the data is completed are known as _____.
9. If data is written on paper before it is entered into the computer, the paper is known as a _____.
10. The five categories of computer hardware are _____, _____, _____, _____, and _____.
11. Data flows from an input device to the _____.
12. Data may flow both directions between the main memory and the _____.

13. Data may flow both directions between the auxiliary storage device and the _____.

14. Data flows from the _____ to an output device.

15. Two commonly used input devices are the _____ and the _____.

16. The processor of a computer may also be referred to as the _____.

17. A processor with all its circuits on one chip is known as a _____.

18. Each location in the memory of the computer is identified by its _____.

19. Memory that "forgets" when the power is turned off is known as _____.

20. Memory that retains its contents even when the power is off is known as _____.

21. The amount of memory needed to store one character is known as a _____.

22. The two most commonly used output devices are _____ and _____.

23. The software that keeps the computer's hardware pieces talking to each other is known as the _____.

24. Routine "housekeeping" jobs are done by _____.

25. Software that solves specific problems for the user is known as _____.

MATCHING EXERCISES

Match the following terms with the clues shown on the following page. Write the letter of each term on the appropriate line. You will not use all of the answers listed since there are more answers than blank lines.

A. byte
B. data
C. floppy
D. program
E. monitor
F. operating system
G. raw
H. printer
I. software or program
J. random access memory
K. processor
L. disk
M. mouse

Name _____ Class _____ Date _____

1. _____ It can be raw but not done.
2. _____ It can be hard but not over easy.
3. _____ It's a "soft" disk.
4. _____ It's a ram but has no horns.
5. _____ Its name implies that it sees things, but it has no sight.
6. _____ Its name says it's soft, but you can't feel it; in fact, you can't even see it.
7. _____ It might be used for "mousing around."
8. _____ You can gulp one character with this.
9. _____ It operates, but not in a hospital.
10. _____ It can be found at a recital as well as in the computer.

IDENTIFICATION QUESTIONS

Label each of the parts in the following pictures as *input device, processor, main memory, auxiliary storage,* or *output device* where the spaces are provided.

1.

Chapter 2 ♦ The Computer System

Name _____ Class _____ Date _____

CROSSWORD PUZZLE

Complete the following Crossword Puzzle. All answers to the puzzle can be found in Chapter 2 of your textbook.

Across Clues
1. the visible parts of a computer system
2. a commonly used input device
5. random access memory
6. an input device that "points"
7. the most commonly used auxiliary storage device
9. an output device that produces permanent copy
10. the amount of storage required to hold one character
12. _____, processing, output
14. memory that retains its contents when the power is turned off
16. instructions a computer follows
17. circuits on a chip
18. software that controls the operation of the hardware

Down Clues
1. an auxiliary storage device that uses a rigid disk
3. input, _____, output
4. information that the user receives
6. the storage locations inside the computer
7. facts
8. a flexible disk
11. used for putting data into the computer
13. a popular display device
15. a set of instructions

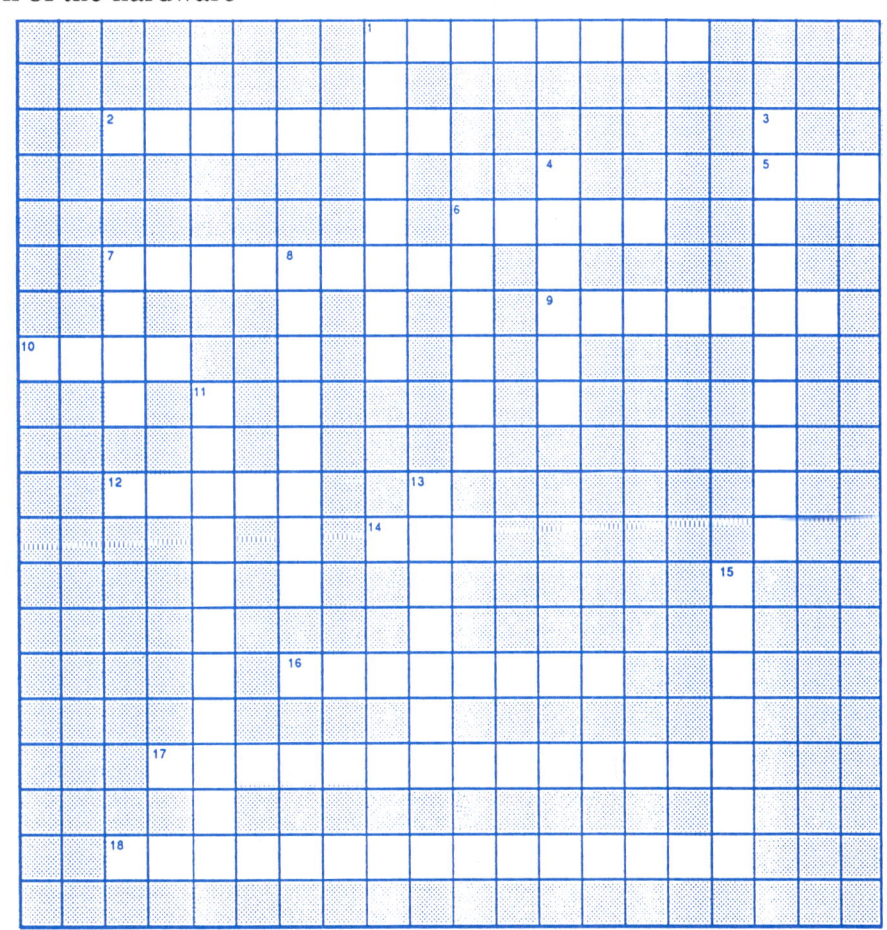

Chapter 2 ♦ The Computer System

11

Name _____ Class _____ Date _____

CHAPTER 3

Word Processing Software

COMPLETION QUESTIONS

1. Software designed to help you write is known as _____.
2. Word processing software uses the standard steps of input, _____, and output.
3. The step of _____ occurs as you enter words on the keyboard, while the step of _____ occurs as you make corrections and revisions.
4. Depending on the program, the word processing function to be performed is selected by entering a _____ or using a _____.
5. An _____ can do other things in addition to word processing.
6. When entering text, you should strike the _____ key only when you want to force a new line.
7. Errors can be corrected by first moving the _____ back to the location of the error.
8. To insert one or more letters into existing text, you should first make sure the word processor's _____ function is turned on.
9. A portion of marked text is known as a _____.
10. Once portions of text are marked, they can be _____, _____, or _____.
11. Cut and paste means the same thing as _____.

13

12. When copied, marked text remains in its old position and is _____ in its new position.
13. To save a document, you first make up a _____ for it.
14. To call a document back into the computer's memory, you use its _____.
15. A spelling checker identifies words that it does not find in its _____.
16. Misspelled words can be replaced automatically by words chosen from the _____.
17. To find the word with the exact meaning you're looking for, you might consult a _____.
18. Definitions are frequently given by a _____ program.
19. Technical checking of a document is done by a _____ program.
20. _____ allows you to print documents for various people, customizing each one with a personal name and address or other information.
21. When customizing the same document for various people, the variable data may come either from the _____ or from a _____.
22. Documents use _____ to indicate the points at which variable data should be inserted.
23. Presaved paragraphs known as _____ may be combined to create new documents customized for their intended use.
24. To create an original layout for material to be printed you could use a _____ program.
25. Three uses of desktop publishing might be _____, _____, or _____.

WORKING AT THE COMPUTER

Complete the following projects. You will need the *Computer Confidence* Template Disk to complete the projects that are marked with a diskette icon.

1. For the word processor you have available for use in your class, write the name of the command or menu choice that is used to complete each of the tasks listed on the next page. If you are using *MicroTools*, follow these steps:

   MicroTools Instructions:

   a. Follow the steps in Appendix A of this workbook for loading *MicroTools* on your computer.

Name _____ Class _____ Date _____

> b. Select Option 1 (Word Processing) from the main menu.
> c. Press <Command><H> to display the Help screen. Use the Help screen to identify the commands or keys used to complete the tasks listed below.

1. Get ready to enter a new document _____
2. Save a document _____
3. Move the cursor left _____
4. Move the cursor right _____
5. Move the cursor up a line _____
6. Move the cursor down a line _____
7. Move the cursor to the beginning of the text _____
8. Move the cursor to the end of the text _____
9. Begin boldface print _____
10. End boldface print _____
11. Begin underlining _____
12. End underlining _____
13. Mark a block of text _____
14. Print a document _____
15. Load a document from the disk _____

2. Using the format shown in Figure 3.4 of your textbook, use the word processor to enter the note given below. Save the note as C3A2XXX (replacing XXX with your initials). Print the note. If you are using *MicroTools* software, use the steps on the following page.

---

318 First Avenue(↵)
Tucson, AZ 98732-3333(↵)
May 18, 19--(↵)
(↵)
(↵)
(↵)
Dear Fran,(↵)
(↵)
I am looking forward to your arrival in Tucson next month. I am planning to take you to Tucson Gardens for a **beautiful** day of water skiing. Then we'll take in the circus that will be performing in the lakefront amphitheater that weekend.(↵)
(↵)
Your friend,(↵)

Figure 3.1
Project 2 Letter

Chapter 3 ♦ Word Processing Software   15

MicroTools Instructions:

a. If the Help screen from Project 1 is still displayed, press the Space Bar to return to the entry screen; if the program is not running, start it up and select the Word Processing option (Option 1) from the opening menu.

b. Enter the note shown in Figure 3.1, using the backspace or cursor keys to back up and correct any mistakes. Strike <Enter/Return> only where the Enter/Return symbol (₋) is shown. Press <Command><B> at the beginning of the boldfaced word; do the same at the end of the word.

c. Save your document. To do this, press <Command><F> for file operations. Then strike <S> for save and enter the following name of the document: C3A2XXX (replacing XXX with your initials).

d. Print your document. First, make sure your printer is ready. Press <Command><P> for print, and strike <P> for printer and <F> for formatted. Then strike <Enter/Return> twice to indicate to the program that you want to start with the first page and continue through the last page.

e. When printing has finished, strike the Space Bar to continue. Then press <Command><Q> to quit the word processor and return to the *MicroTools* main menu. Press <Esc> to leave the program.

3. Load the note you created in Project 2. Add a second paragraph that says "Please let me know your airline and flight number so I can pick you up. The airport is only 20 minutes from my home." Then save and print the note (use C3A3XXX as the new filename). The *MicroTools* steps are as follows:

MicroTools Instructions:

a. Start the program and select the Word Processing option (Option 1) from the main menu.

b. Press <Command><F> for file operations. Then strike <L> to load a file. Use the cursor keys to highlight C3A2XXX and press <Enter/Return> to load the file.

c. When the document appears on the screen, use the cursor keys to move the cursor to the point currently occupied by the Y in "Your friend."

d. Make sure the word INSERT appears in the top right of the screen. If it does not, press <Insert> to make it appear. If your computer does not have an Insert key, press <Command><O> to toggle (switch) from overstrike to insert mode.

e. Key in the new paragraph, correcting any errors.

f. Press <Command><F> for file operations. Then strike

Name _____ Class _____ Date _____

> <S> for save; the name C3A2XXX will appear. Save the document as C3A3XXX.
>
> g. Press <Command><P> for print. Then strike <P> for printer and <F> for formatted and strike <Enter/Return> twice to indicate start printing at the first page and continue through the last page.
>
> h. After printing is complete, strike the Space Bar. Press <Command><Q> to quit the word processor. Press <Esc> to exit *MicroTools*.

4. One of the most used features of word processing software is the ability to make corrections to a document. This allows the user to concentrate on getting his or her thoughts into the computer without being overly concerned about grammar, spelling, and punctuation. Then, once the thoughts are on paper (or on the screen), the user can go back and make corrections, both to smooth the flow of the thoughts and to clean up the grammar, spelling, and punctuation.

On the template disk is a file named C3A4 which contains just such a document. This document is shown in Figure 3.2.

The Henrysville School Board announced today that the new shcool to be constructed by the district wiil set new standards of quality in the state. The details were given by Dr. Wanda marietta, Superintendetn.

At the heart of the plans is a stresss on developing the well-rounded student; both educationally and physically. The education progarm of the shcool stress problem-solving capability rather than just having students memorize content. Such problem-solving ability has been shown to be a necessary element for studnets to succeed in the world of work.

While learning the traditional subjects is certainly stressed in the school, the physical side is also considered important. This will be the first school in the state to contain an Olympic-sized indoor swimming pool. This pool will help students develop a recreatinoal skill they can for life.

The new school to be named L Logan Mayes High is creating such excitemnt in the educational community that teams of visitors from other states are already signing up for visits.

Figure 3.2
File C3A4

The writer used the word processor to get the thoughts recorded. Now it is your job to refine the document. The document has at least one incomplete sentence, at least one incorrect instance of punctuation, at least one instance of subject-verb disagreement, and several misspelled words. Load the document from the template disk and then save it back to your data disk using

Chapter 3 ♦ Word Processing Software

C3A4XXX (replacing XXX in the filename with your initials) as the name of the document. After saving the document under the new name, correct all the errors that you find. Save the corrected document (again using C3A4XXX as the filename) and print a copy of it.

> *MicroTools* Instructions:
>
> a. Follow the instructions in Appendix A of your workbook to load *MicroTools*.
>
> b. Select the Word Processor option (Option 1) from the main menu.
>
> c. Once the word processor has been loaded, press <Command><F> to begin the File Operations command. Press <L> to load a document. A list of available documents will appear on your screen. Use the cursor keys to highlight **C3A4**. Press <Enter/Return> to load the document.
>
> d. Save the document back to your disk using C3A4XXX (replacing XXX with your initials). For example, if your name is Kelly Helen Rockmoor, you would use the filename C3A4KHR. To save the document, press <Command><F> to begin the File Operations command, and press <S> to save the document. Enter *C3A4XXX* as the new filename. By performing this step, you will have created a copy of the original document on disk. The text of the document will still be in memory for you to complete the activity.
>
> e. Use the cursor control keys to move to the places you want to make corrections. Then key in the corrections.
>
> f. Save your document under its default filename, which is now C3A4XXX. To do this, press <Command><F>, and then press <S> for Save. When the default filename of C3A4XXX appears, press <Enter/Return> to save the document using that name.
>
> g. Press <Command><P> to print a copy of the modified document. If a printer is attached to your computer, press <P> to print the document to the printer; otherwise, press <S> to print the document to the screen. Press <F> to print a formatted version of the document. Press <Enter/Return> two times to print the entire document.
>
> h. Press <Command><Q> to quit the word processing program. Press <Esc> to exit the *MicroTools* program.

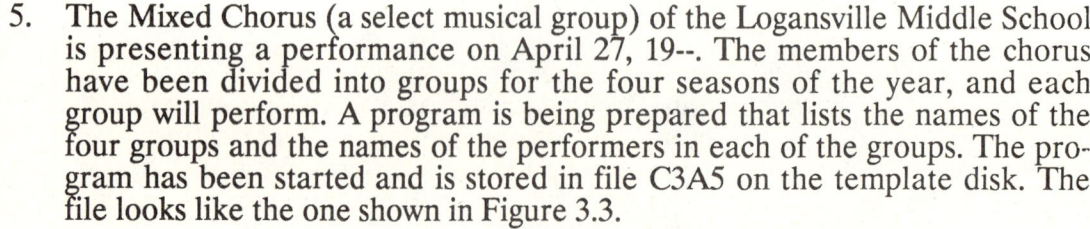

5. The Mixed Chorus (a select musical group) of the Logansville Middle School is presenting a performance on April 27, 19--. The members of the chorus have been divided into groups for the four seasons of the year, and each group will perform. A program is being prepared that lists the names of the four groups and the names of the performers in each of the groups. The program has been started and is stored in file C3A5 on the template disk. The file looks like the one shown in Figure 3.3.

Name _____ Class _____ Date _____

> The Mixed Chorus of Logansville Middle School presents SEASONS!
> April 27, 19--
> Winter
> Isaac Morgan
> Wilhelmina March
> Lu Wan
> Summer
> Jack Rachels
> Willy Eubanks
> Susan Strimark
> Lea Logan
> Spring
> Joseph Wommack
> Jose Rodriguez
> Loman Blackman
> Linda Lumbard
> Fall
> Sallylu Lairsey
> April Keischein
> Michelle Marchbank
> Boz Hardin

Figure 3.3
File C3A5

You should load the file from the template disk and then store it back to your data disk using the name C3A5XXX. You will notice that the seasons are not given in order. Put the seasons in order by marking a season name and its performers as a block, and then moving the block of text to the correct location. It doesn't matter which season you decide to put first, but after that they should appear in the order they occur.

Once you have put the seasons in correct order, work with margins and placement of the words on the page to make it look good. Just use your creativity and judgment. After making these format changes, save the document to disk as C3A5XXX. Print a copy of the program.

> *MicroTools* Instructions:
>
> a. Load the *MicroTools* software. (Refer to the start-up procedures in Appendix A if you need help.) Select Option 1 from the main menu to load the word processor.
>
> b. Press <Command><F> to begin the File Operations command, and press <L> for load. Use the cursor keys to highlight file C3A5 and press <Enter/Return> to load the file.
>
> c. To save the file under its new name, press <Command><F> to begin the File Operations command. Press <S> for save, and key the new filename

Chapter 3 ♦ Word Processing Software

(C3A5XXX). Press <Enter/Return> to complete the command.

d. Select a season that needs to be moved. For example, if you want the program to start with winter, select the season of spring so that you can move it between winter and summer. Move the cursor to the first letter of the name of the season. Press <Command><M> to begin marking the block to be moved. Next, move the cursor to the end of the block to be moved and press <Enter/Return>. The following prompt will appear on your screen:

Copy, Delete, Move, or Save?
Select block operation by keying first letter.

---

e. Press <M> to move the block. The following prompt will appear on your screen:

Move the cursor to the new location, then press ENTER.

---

f. Move the cursor to the <Enter/Return> symbol before the new location for the block, and then press <Enter/Return>. Press <Enter/Return> again to add a carriage return.

g. Repeat steps d-f until the program is arranged the way you want it.

h. Use margin and centering commands to make the program page look nice and easy to read. If you need assistance using these commands, refer to the Help screen.

i. Save the program using the default name of C3A5XXX.

j. Print the program.

k. Exit the word processor and *MicroTools*.

CROSSWORD PUZZLE

Complete the following Crossword Puzzle. All answers to the puzzle can be found in Chapter 3 of your textbook.

Across Clues
1. software that can perform several major activities
4. any marked portion of text
5. stand-in words that are replaced at print time
6. indicates point on the screen at which next letter will be displayed
8. helps to find misspelled words
9. makes arrangements of text and graphics on page for printing
10. used for entering, revising, and printing text

Down Clues
2. helps to find synonyms
3. assembling documents from presaved paragraphs
4. presaved paragraphs that are assembled
6. another term for moving text
7. puts variable values in documents at print time

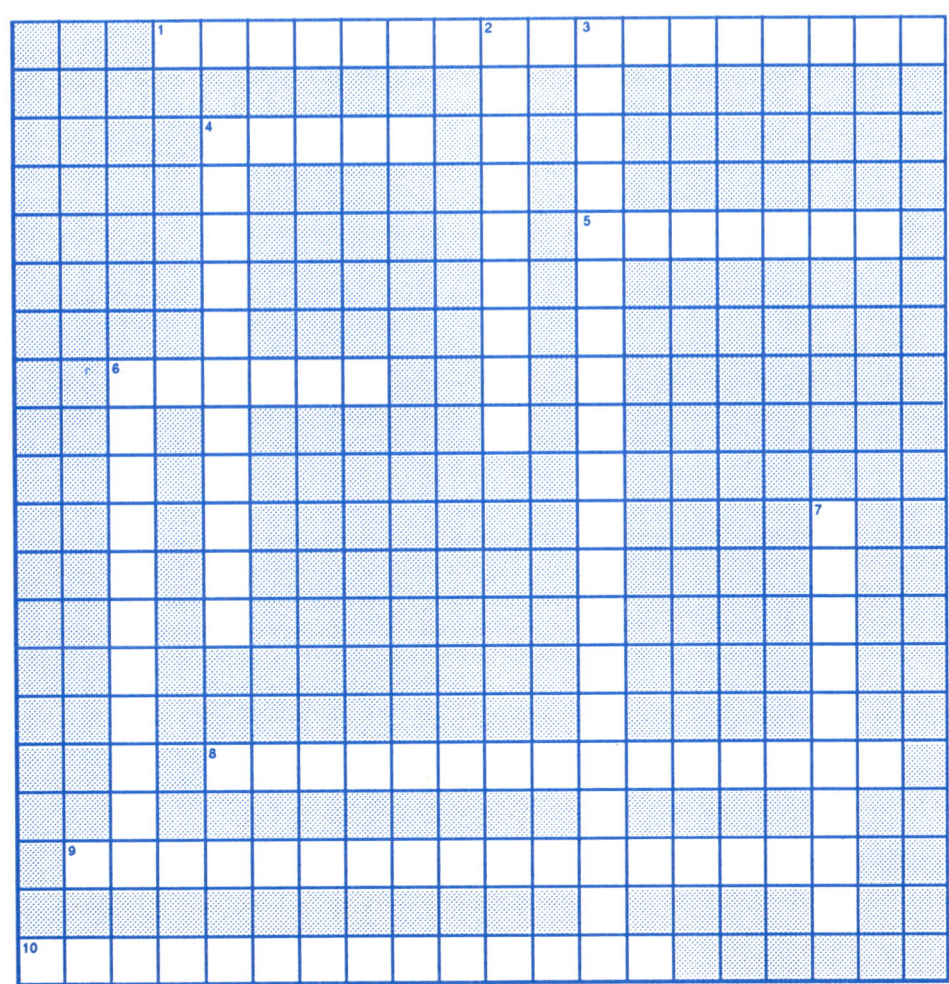

Chapter 3 ♦ Word Processing Software

Name _____ Class _____ Date _____

CHAPTER 4

Spreadsheet Software

COMPLETION QUESTIONS

1. A table of data may be known as a _____.
2. A horizontal line of data on a spreadsheet is known as a _____ and is identified by a _____.
3. A vertical line of data on a spreadsheet is known as a _____ and is identified by a _____.
4. A cell is identified by its _____ number and _____ letter.
5. The highlighted rectangle indicating the cell into which an item will be keyed is known as the _____.
6. When alphabetic data is wider than the cell into which it is entered, it may extend over the cells to the right if they have _____ in them.
7. Alphabetic data entered into a spreadsheet is known as a _____.
8. The column width that is used unless you specify otherwise is known as the _____ width.
9. To lessen the amount of loss if a power failure or equipment failure occurs, you should _____ your spreadsheet at regular intervals.
10. The instructions on how to do a mathematical computation are known as a _____.

23

11. When a formula is entered into a cell and <Enter/Return> or a cursor key is struck, the _____ of the computation appears in the cell.

12. Formulas may use just about any combination of cell _____, math _____, and _____.

13. Two functions that may be used are _____ and _____.

14. To avoid rekeying a formula in a second location, you may _____ it from one cell to another.

15. When a formula is copied, the cell references in it may be _____ to reflect its new position in the spreadsheet.

16. A cell reference that will automatically update when the formula is copied is known as a _____ reference.

17. A cell reference that does not update when the formula is copied is known as an _____ reference.

18. When scrolling a spreadsheet, the image you see can be thought of as being seen through a _____.

19. The _____ of the rows and columns can be commanded to stay on the screen while the data scrolls on and off the screen.

20. Two categories of spreadsheet applications are _____ spreadsheets and _____ spreadsheets.

MATCHING EXERCISES

Match the following terms with their clues. Write the letter of each term on the appropriate line.

A. column
B. relative reference
C. cell
D. scroll
E. absolute reference
F. cell pointer
G. default
H. row
I. function
J. label

1. _____ I'm the smallest building block of a spreadsheet just as of a living organism.
2. _____ I once held up the roof of a Greek building, but now I hold data.
3. _____ I don't point to a place in prison but to a place in a spreadsheet.
4. _____ This reference doesn't tell an employer all about my good points for a job, but it is just as unchanging as they are.
5. _____ I don't say bad things about my kin, but I'm very changeable.

Name _____ Class _____ Date _____

6. _____ I'm not a missed payment, but I am used when no instructions are given.
7. _____ Where my ancestors rolled, I move side to side or up and down.
8. _____ You can find me in a stadium or on a spreadsheet.
9. _____ I answer the "what is it?" riddle.
10. _____ I work hard and am not lazy, but my user may be.

IDENTIFICATION QUESTIONS

The following spreadsheet contains hidden messages. Decode each message that follows it by looking at each referenced cell in the spreadsheet and writing down the letter you find. The first two letters are given to illustrate the process.

	A	B	C	D	E	F	G	H	I	J	K	L	M	N	O	P	Q	R
1	U	X	R	O	Z	Y	M	A	B	F	G	H	T	U	M	X	R	C
2	O	Y	C	E	A	I	K	X	Y	C	E	I	O	A	P	O	R	X
3	A	B	L	E	M	C	E	L	L	O	W	E	C	A	E	U	O	N
4	N	I	W	C	O	L	U	M	N	R	O	W	P	O	I	N	T	W
5	C	F	F	L	A	P	O	Y	E	Q	E	F	W	D	W	O	I	E
6	I	O	O	D	E	F	A	U	L	T	I	W	O	3	8	S	O	W
7	A	C	F	U	N	C	T	I	O	L	U	I	N	A	L	E	1	D
8	I	O	A	E	O	I	W	D	Y	I	E	P	W	Q	T	C	V	D
9	Y	T	D	S	A	B	S	O	L	U	T	E	O	N	L	Y	C	S
10	N	,	D	D	S	D	S	S	S	L	A	B	E	L	I	W	A	
11	R	E	L	A	T	I	V	E	R	E	F	E	R	E	N	C	E	A
12	I	G	A	R	C	U	A	C	M	N	I	W	A	E	O	I	S	N

                  H5   M9   A1   C5..C6   P3   R12   F10   E3   K2

Message 1   Y   O   __   __   __   __   __   __   __   __

                  B12   M9   C6   R8   J7..K7   R1   G2

Message 2   __   __   __   __   __   __   __

WORKING AT THE COMPUTER

Complete the following projects. You will need the *Computer Confidence Template Disk* to complete the projects that are marked with a diskette icon.

Chapter 4 ♦ Spreadsheet Software

1. For the spreadsheet program you have available for use in your class, write the name of the command or menu choice that is used to complete each of the tasks below. If you are using *MicroTools*, follow these steps:

   > *MicroTools* Instructions:
   >
   > a. Follow the steps in Appendix A of this workbook for loading *MicroTools* on your computer.
   >
   > b. Select Option 2 (Spreadsheet) from the main menu.
   >
   > c. Press <Command><H> to display the Help screen. Use the Help screen to identify the commands or keys used to complete the tasks listed below.

   1. Start a new spreadsheet _____
   2. Save a spreadsheet _____
   3. Load a spreadsheet from the disk _____
   4. Move the cell pointer left _____
   5. Move the cell pointer right _____
   6. Move the cell pointer up a line _____
   7. Move the cell pointer down a line _____
   8. Move the cell pointer to the beginning of the spreadsheet _____
   9. Move the cell pointer to the end of the spreadsheet _____
   10. Print the spreadsheet _____

2. Enter, save, and print the spreadsheet shown in Figure 4.1. Put your name in Cell A2. Save the file as C4A2XXX. If you are using the *MicroTools* spreadsheet, use the steps provided on the next page.

	A	B	C	D	E
1:	Votes Cast for Student Body President				
2:					
3:		Tenth	Eleventh	Twelfth	Totals
4:	Brady	132.00	117.00	96.00	345.00
5:	Johnson	96.00	102.00	112.00	310.00
6:					

   Figure 4.1
   Project 2 Spreadsheet

Name _____ Class _____ Date _____

MicroTools Instructions:

a. If the Help screen from Project 1 is still displayed, press the Space Bar to return to the entry screen; if the program is not running, start it up and select the Spreadsheet option (Option 2) from the opening menu.

b. Using the cursor control keys to move the cell pointer to the illustrated cells, enter the labels and values into the cells shown in Figure 4.1. If you make a mistake before striking <Enter/Return> or a cursor key, backspace and correct it. If you realize later that you made a mistake, move the cell pointer back to the cell and rekey the contents correctly. Enter a quotation mark at the beginning of Tenth, Eleventh, Twelfth, and Totals to make the labels align at the right edge of the cell. Do not enter the values in cells E4 and E5. You will use a formula to calculate the totals. Enter your name in Cell A2.

c. Enter a formula to calculate the total votes received by Brady. Move the cell pointer to Cell E4, key in @SUM(B4..D4) and strike <Enter/Return>. The total of 345 will appear in the cell. Another formula that works just as well is +B4+C4+D4.

d. Copy the formula from Cell E4 to Cell E5 for Johnson. Make sure the cell pointer is on Cell E4, and press <Command><C> for copy. The following prompt will appear:

Put cursor at the end of the block to be copied, then press ENTER.

Since Cell E4 is the only cell to be copied, press <Enter/Return>. The following prompt will appear:

Enter destination cell name: (A1-Z64)_

Key in the destination cell name of E5 and strike <Enter/Return>. The total of 310 for Johnson will appear in the cell.

e. When you are finished entering the labels and values, press <Command><F> (for file operations) and then press <S> to save your spreadsheet. Key in a filename of C4A2XXX (replacing XXX with your initials). For example, if your initials are SAC, key in the name C4A2SAC and strike <Enter/Return>. This will save the spreadsheet.

f. Print the spreadsheet by pressing <Command><P>, and then striking <P> for printer. Press <P> to print the spreadsheet "as is."

g. Quit the spreadsheet program by pressing <Command><Q> for quit.

Chapter 4 ♦ Spreadsheet Software

3. On the template disk, file C4A3 contains a spreadsheet showing the grades of students in a class. The spreadsheet looks like the one shown in Figure 4.2.

```
         A                B           C           D           E
 1: (Student's Name)
 2: Grades for Science 720--Ms. Johnstone
 3:
 4: Name             Test 1      Test 2      Test 3      Average
 5:
 6: Adams, G.          95          90          85
 7: Bryant, H.         85          90          90
 8: Fehnmann, R.       75          80          80
 9: Mimms, H.          85          80          85
10: Sargent, A.        95          90          95
11: Wyko, S.           90          95          90
12: Zarman, W.         80          85          85
```

Figure 4.2
File C4A3

Load the file, and save it under the name C4A3XXX (replacing XXX with your initials). In Cell E6 enter a formula that will average the first student's grades. Then copy that formula down for the other students. Save the modified spreadsheet and print out a copy showing the students' averages.

MicroTools Instructions:

a. Follow the instructions in Appendix A of your workbook to load *MicroTools*.

b. Select the Spreadsheet option (Option 2) from the main menu.

c. Once the spreadsheet has been loaded, press <Command><F> to begin the File Operations command. Press <L> to load a spreadsheet. A list of available spreadsheets will appear on your screen. Use the cursor keys to highlight C4A3. Press <Enter/Return> to load the file.

d. Move the cell pointer to Cell A1 and enter your name.

e. Use the cursor keys to move the cell pointer to Cell E6. Key in the following formula to compute the average for the first student: @SUM(B6..D6)/@COUNT(B6..D6)

f. To copy the formula to each of the following students, first move the cursor to the cell to be copied (E6). Press <Command><C> to begin the Copy command. The following prompt will appear on your screen:

28 Workbook ♦ *Computer Confidence: A Challenge for Today*

Put cursor at the end of the block to be copied, then press ENTER.

g. Since the cursor is already at the end of the block to be copied, press <Enter/Return>. The following prompt will appear on your screen:

Enter destination cell name: (A1-Z64) _

h. Enter *E7* as the destination cell name. The formula will be copied to Cell E7, and an average will be computed for the student in Row 7. If you move your cursor to Cell E7, you will notice that the formula has automatically been updated to read *@SUM(B7..D7)/@COUNT(B7..D7)*. Since relative cell references were used, the spreadsheet program knew to modify the formula to average the test scores in Row 7 instead of those in Row 6.

i. Repeat Steps f-h to copy the formula to the remaining rows. You can copy more than one cell at a time by marking more than one cell to be copied. For example, when the prompt in Step f appears, move the cursor down to Cell E7 before pressing <Enter/Return>. When E8 is entered as the destination cell, the formula will be copied to both Cells E8 and E9.

j. Save the spreadsheet using its default name of C4A3XXX.

k. Begin the Print command by pressing <Command><P>. Press <P> to print to the printer, and then press <P> to print the spreadsheet "as is."

l. Press <Command><Q> to quit the spreadsheet. Press <Esc> to exit the *MicroTools* program.

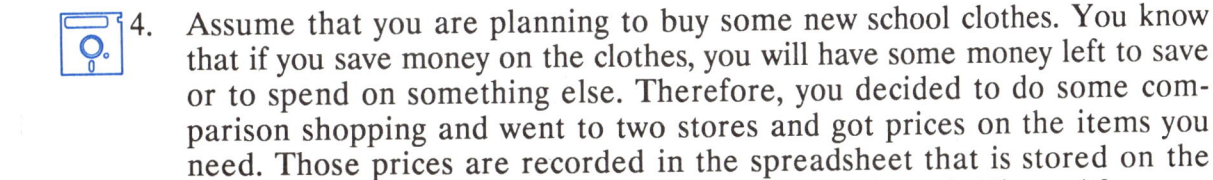

4. Assume that you are planning to buy some new school clothes. You know that if you save money on the clothes, you will have some money left to save or to spend on something else. Therefore, you decided to do some comparison shopping and went to two stores and got prices on the items you need. Those prices are recorded in the spreadsheet that is stored on the template disk as C4A4. The file looks like the one shown in Figure 4.3.

After putting the data in the spreadsheet, you decide to add the prices from another store, Megan's, to your comparison. Therefore, load the spreadsheet from the template disk, and save it to your data disk under the name

Chapter 4 ♦ Spreadsheet Software

	A	B	C	D	E
1:	(Student's Name)				
2:	School Clothes Price Comparison				
3:					
4:	Item	Aaron's	Xantho's		
5:					
6:	Jeans, #1	39.95	34.95		
7:	Jeans, #2	37.95	38.95		
8:	Shirt, Red	27.95	29.95		
9:	Shirt, Yellow	19.95	18.95		
10:	Shirt, Blue	24.50	24.85		
11:	Socks, 4 pr.	9.95	8.75		
12:					
13:					

Figure 4.3
File C4A4

C4A4XXX (replacing XXX with your initials). Insert a column in the spreadsheet between Columns B and C for Megan's (to keep the stores in alphabetic order), and enter the following prices in the column:

Jeans, #1: 39.95
Jeans, #2: 38.95
Shirt, Red: 25.95
Shirt, Yellow: 26.95
Shirt, Blue: 23.95
Socks, 4 pr.: 12.50

Then, to give yourself a better idea of how the prices compare, sum the columns for each store. This will show you which store has the lowest total price if you buy everything at the same store.

Next, add a new column to the right of the other columns. In this column you should enter the lowest price of the three for each item. Also sum this new column to see how much you will spend if you go to more than one store, getting the lowest possible price on each item.

After adding the new columns and data, save the spreadsheet and print a copy of it.

MicroTools Instructions:

a. Load *MicroTools*. (Refer to the start-up procedures in Appendix A if you need help.) Select Option 2 from the main menu to load the spreadsheet.

b. Press <Command><F> to begin the File Operations command. Press <L> to load a file. Use the cursor keys to highlight C4A4 and press <Enter/Return> to load the file.

c. To save the file under its new name, press <Command><F> to begin the File Operations command. Press <S> for save, and then key the new filename (C4A4XXX). Press <Enter/Return> to complete the command.

d. Move the cursor to Cell A1 and enter your name.

e. Move the cursor keys to any cell in Column C. Press <Command><I> to insert a new column. The following prompt will appear on your screen:

Insert column or row? (c or r) _

---

f. Press <C> to insert a new column. The following prompt will appear on your screen:

Insert column? (A-Z) C

---

g. Press <Enter/Return> to accept the default value of C as the column to insert. This will cause the spreadsheet to insert a column between Columns B and C.

h. Move the cursor to Cell C4 and enter the following label: *"Megan's*. (Keying a quotation mark in front of the label makes it line up at the right of the column.) Then enter the new prices in the appropriate cells.

i. Move the cursor to Cell A13 and enter the following heading: *Totals*.

j. In Cell B13, enter the following formula: *@SUM(B6..B11)* Then copy this formula to Cells C13 and D13.

k. Move the cursor to Cell E4 and enter the following heading: *"Lowest*.

l. In Cells E6 through E11, enter the lowest price for each item. For example, Xantho's has the lowest price for Jeans, #1. Therefore, enter *34.95* in Cell E6.

m. Enter a formula in Cell E13 to sum the amounts in Column E. (As an alternative, you may copy the formula from Cell D13 to Cell E13.)

n. To save the spreadsheet, press <Command><F> to begin the File Operations command. Then press <S> for save, and press <Enter/Return> to accept the default filename of C4A4XXX.

o. Press <Command><P> to print the spreadsheet. Press <P> to print the spreadsheet to the printer. Press <P> to print the spreadsheet "as is."

p. Press <Command><Q> to quit the spreadsheet program. Press <Esc> to exit *MicroTools*.

Chapter 4 ♦ Spreadsheet Software

CROSSWORD PUZZLE

Complete the following Crossword Puzzle. All answers to the puzzle can be found in Chapter 4 of your textbook.

Across Clues
4. indicates cell into which data will be keyed
7. kind of reference that will not change when a formula is copied
8. what is used if you don't specify anything
12. something the spreadsheet knows how to do
13. kind of reference that updates when a formula is copied
14. kind of spreadsheet that tries to predict the future

Down Clues
1. key used to move the cell pointer
2. cell to which a formula is copied
3. a vertical area
4. the place that holds one value
5. a word on a spreadsheet
6. a horizontal area
9. math instructions
10. kind of spreadsheet that describes things that have already happened
11. move sideways or up and down

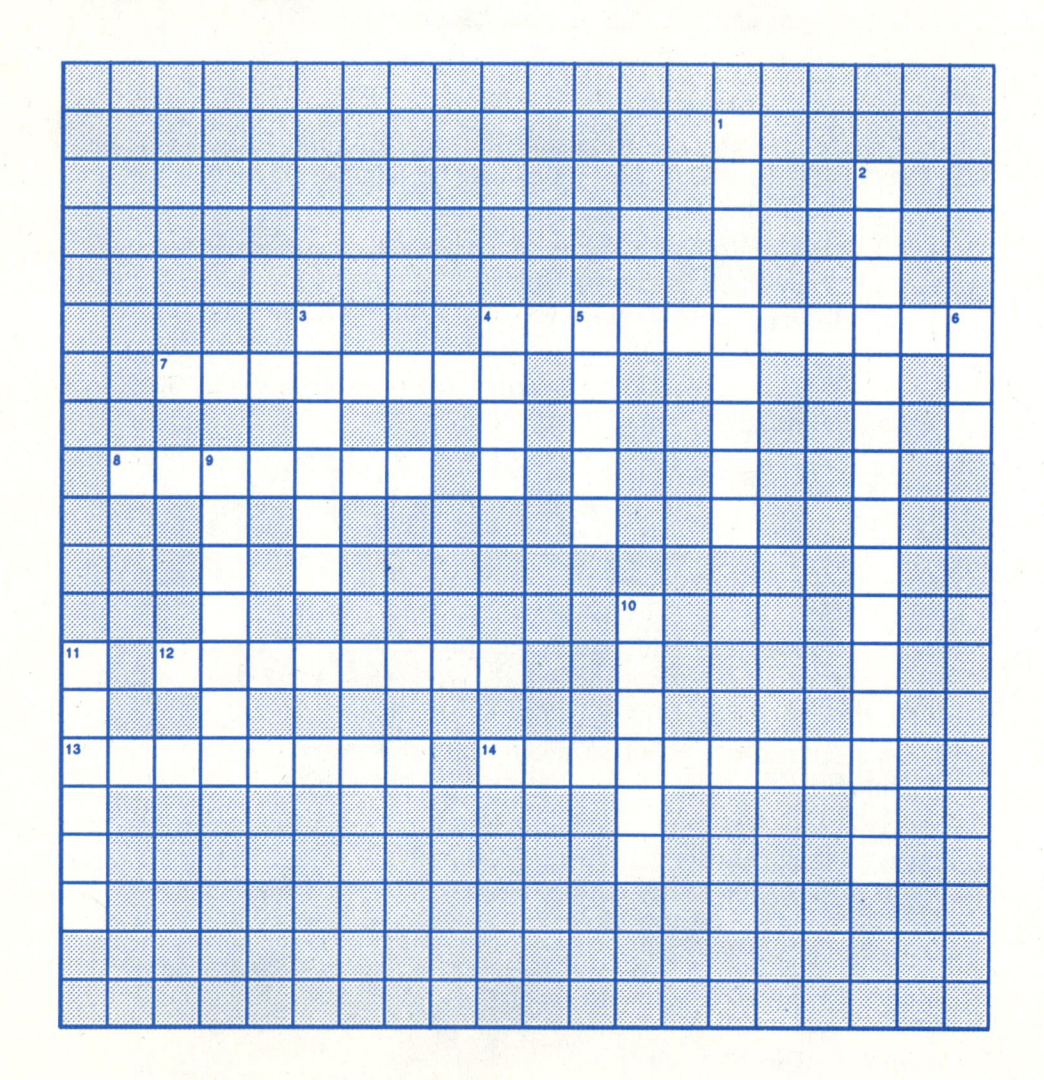

Name _____ Class _____ Date _____

CHAPTER 5

Database Software

COMPLETION QUESTIONS

1. A collection of data about items that are part of a group is known as a _____.

2. Four examples of databases are your teacher's _____, a collection of _____ for a cook, the _____ of a library, and your personal address list.

3. All the data recorded about one item (such as one book or one person) is known as a _____.

4. Each different kind of data recorded about one item is known as a _____.

5. The first step in planning a database is to decide the _____ of the database.

6. The second step in planning a database is to decide what _____ are to be included.

7. After deciding the names of fields, you decide how _____ the fields are and what kind of _____ they are to hold.

8. The field lengths of the database should be as _____ as possible while still allowing the data to be as complete and meaningful as necessary.

9. Designating a data field as _____ or _____ determines whether you can do arithmetic with the field.

33

10. After naming a new database to the computer, you enter the name of each _____, its length, and the kind of data it is to hold.

11. Adding data to a database is known as _____ or _____.

12. The real power of a database program is its ability to _____ the data to come up with the desired information.

13. Usually a record is removed by first displaying it, then giving a command to _____ it.

14. The process of arranging records in a desired order is known as _____.

15. Sorting may be done on different _____ depending on the needs of the user.

16. Sorts may usually be done in either _____ or _____ order.

17. With some database software, the program is capable of doing _____ to come up with counts or totals.

18. When _____ on paper, the records of a database may be arranged in the desired order.

19. When printing, you may have a _____ in effect so that only selected records will print.

20. With many database programs, you can specify which _____ will print on a report.

IDENTIFICATION QUESTIONS

For each of the following activities, enter the letter of its description: A=arrange data, C=create database, D=delete data, E=edit data, I=insert data, P=print data, S=select or search data. Some activities may need two letters if two operations are being used.

1. _____ A school club wants to keep records of its members.
2. _____ The school counselor needs to add a new student who has just enrolled to the database.
3. _____ The school needs mailing labels to send newsletters to all parents whose names and addresses are already in the database.
4. _____ The school needs to know which students made the honor roll.
5. _____ The end of the school year has arrived and students who have left the school need to be removed from the database.
6. _____ A student has a new telephone number which must replace the old number in the database.

Name _____ Class _____ Date _____

7. _____ Each teacher needs to look at records in the database only for his or her own students.
8. _____ Student records already in the database need to be looked at alphabetically.
9. _____ All the students in Mr. Branch's class need to be listed on a printout.
10. _____ A directory of students already in the database needs to be printed in alphabetic order.

WORKING AT THE COMPUTER

Complete the following projects. You will need the *Computer Confidence* Template Disk to complete the projects that are marked with a diskette icon.

1. For the database program you have available, write the name of the command or menu choice that is used to do each of the following steps. If you are using the *MicroTools* software, follow the steps below to help you find the answers. If you are using other software, the answers will be different.

    a. Start the database program _____
    b. Create a new database _____
    c. Use an existing database _____
    d. Add a new record _____
    e. Find an existing record _____
    f. Go to the next record _____
    g. Go to the previous record _____
    h. Sort records into order _____
    i. Print a record _____
    j. Print a report _____
    k. Save changes made in a record _____
    l. Save the database to disk _____

    MicroTools Instructions:

    a. Follow the steps in Appendix A of this workbook for loading *MicroTools* on your computer.
    b. Select Option 3 (Database) from the main menu.
    c. Enter <L> to load an existing database. Highlight File C7A1 and press <Enter/Return>.
    d. Press <Command><H> to display the Help screen. Use the Help screen to identify the commands or keys used to complete the tasks listed.
    e. Quit the Database and return to the Main Menu.

Chapter 5 ♦ Database Software

2. Create a database to use in examining the academic performance of students. Use the following fields:

   Last Name, 15 characters, alphabetic
   First Name, 15 characters, alphabetic,
   Class, 2 digits, numeric
   GPA, 1 digit to left of decimal, 3 to right, numeric

   > *MicroTools* Instructions:
   >
   > a. Select Option 3 (Database) from the main menu.
   > b. Enter <M> to make a new database.
   > c. Enter a name of GPA for the new database.
   > d. When the screen below appears, indicate a size of 60 records by entering the appropriate letter.

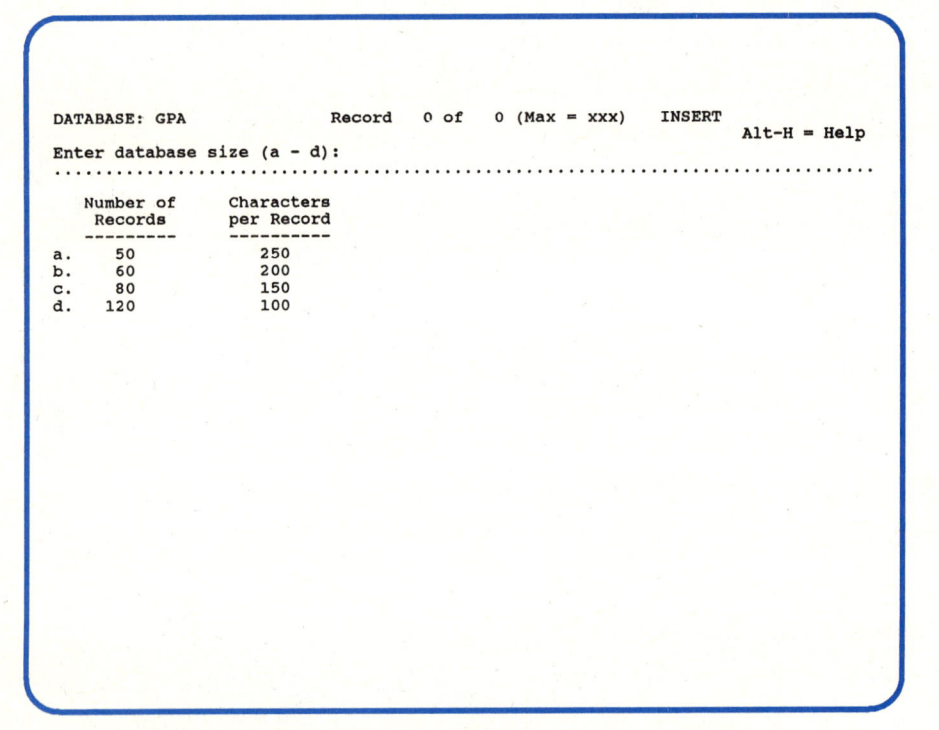

   ```
   DATABASE: GPA              Record   0 of   0 (Max = xxx)   INSERT
                                                              Alt-H = Help
   Enter database size (a - d):
   ...........................................................................

           Number of      Characters
           Records        per Record
           --------       ----------
   a.      50             250
   b.      60             200
   c.      80             150
   d.      120            100
   ```

   * The screen shown is for the IBM version of MicroTools.

   > e. Enter <4> as the number of fields per record.
   > f. Enter the label (name), length, and type (alphabetic or numeric) for each field (as shown on the next page). The length for the GPA field will be entered as 5 (1 space for the digit to the left of the decimal, plus 1 space for the decimal, plus 3 spaces to the right of the decimal).

36   Workbook ♦ *Computer Confidence: A Challenge for Today*

```
DATABASE: GPA              Record   1 of   0 (Max =  50)   INSERT        CAPS
                                                                  Alt-H = Help
Are the field labels, lengths, and types all correct? (y or n)
................................................................................
1: [LAST NAME  ]    [15]      [A]
2: [FIRST NAME]    [15]      [A]
3: [CLASS     ]    [2 ]      [N]
4: [GPA       ]    [5 ]      [N]
```

g. When you are finished entering the labels, lengths, and types, check all the data to make sure you entered it correctly. If you detect an error, correct it. When all the data is correct, press <Enter> until you reach the end and press <Y> to answer the question "Are all the field labels, lengths, and types correct?"

h. When the data entry screen appears, enter the following records. Press <Command><K> (for keep) after each record to keep the data.

   Sam Jones, Grade 10, GPA 4.000

   Brenda Ryan, Grade 10, GPA 3.500

   Larry Bryan, Grade 9, GPA 2.300

   Yvonne Abel, Grade 10, GPA 3.873

i. Press <Command><F>, then <S> to save the database, and then enter the name C5A2XXX. Your screen will look like the illustration shown at the top of the next page.

j. Press <Command><Q> to quit the database, and then <Esc> to leave the *MicroTools* software.

Chapter 5 ♦ Database Software

```
DATABASE: GPA                Record   1 of   7 (Max =  50)   INSERT
                                                              Alt-H = Help
Save database as: GPA
................................................................................
 1: Last Name   [Abel            ]
 2: First Name  [Yvonne          ]
 3: Class       [10]
 4: GPA         [3.873]
```

3. Add new data to your existing database.

   MicroTools Instructions:

   a. Load your database program again. Select Option 3 from the *MicroTools* main menu, then <L> for load existing database. Select C5A2XXX by using the up or down arrow keys to highlight it on the list of files that appears. Then strike <Enter> to select the database.

   b. Press <Command><I> to insert a new record in the database. Then add the following persons to your database. Remember to enter <Command><K> after each person to keep the data.

   > Raymond Markson, Grade 8, GPA 3.125
   > Tien Shih, Grade 9, GPA 3.950
   > Rhonda Lacey, Grade 10, GPA 3.100

   c. Press <Command><F> and then <S> to save the database.

4. Work with existing data in the database.

   MicroTools Instructions:

   a. If you left the database program after Step 3, reload the database.

> b. Find Larry Bryan's record by pressing <Command><S> for search, <E> for equal to, and <1> for Field 1 (last name). Then enter **Bryan**. To also search by first name, enter <A> for and, <E> for equal to, <2> for Field 2 (first name), and then enter **Larry**. The record will appear on the screen.
>
> c. Print Larry's record by entering <Command><P>.
>
> d. Press <Command> <C> to cancel the search criteria.

5. Print an alphabetic report of all data in the database.

   > *MicroTools* Instructions:
   >
   > a. Arrange the data alphabetically by pressing <Command><A> for arrange. Then enter <1> for Field 1 (last name) and <A> for ascending.
   >
   > b. Press <Command><R> for report, then **S** for standard.
   >
   > c. In the form that appears on the screen, enter 1, 2, 3, 4 to indicate the order in which the fields should appear on the report. Then enter <Y> to verify that the order is correct.

   ```
   DATABASE: GPA              Record   1 of   7 (Max =  50)   INSERT
                                                              Alt-H = Help
   Enter 1 for first field to be printed, 2 for second, etc.  Report width: 42
   ..............................................................
       1: Last Name   15 characters     [1 ]
       2: First Name  15 characters     [2 ]
       3:     Class    2 characters     [3 ]
       4:       GPA    5 characters     [4 ]
   ```

   > d. Press <P> to send output to the printer. The report will be printed.

6. Save the database to disk and exit the program.

Chapter 5 ♦ Database Software

CROSSWORD PUZZLE

Complete the following Crossword Puzzle. All answers to the puzzle can be found in Chapter 5 of your textbook.

Across Clues
2. the information about one item
5. adding new records
7. from smallest to largest
8. ach kind of data recorded about an item
11. looking for the desired record
13. removing a record from a database
14. < >
15. where you find the rules for naming fields
16. > =

Down Clues
1. arranging records in order
3. a collection of records
4. what you do before describing the database to the computer
6. the number of characters in a field
8. from largest to smallest
10. another name for field
12. the kind of arithmetic that adds things up

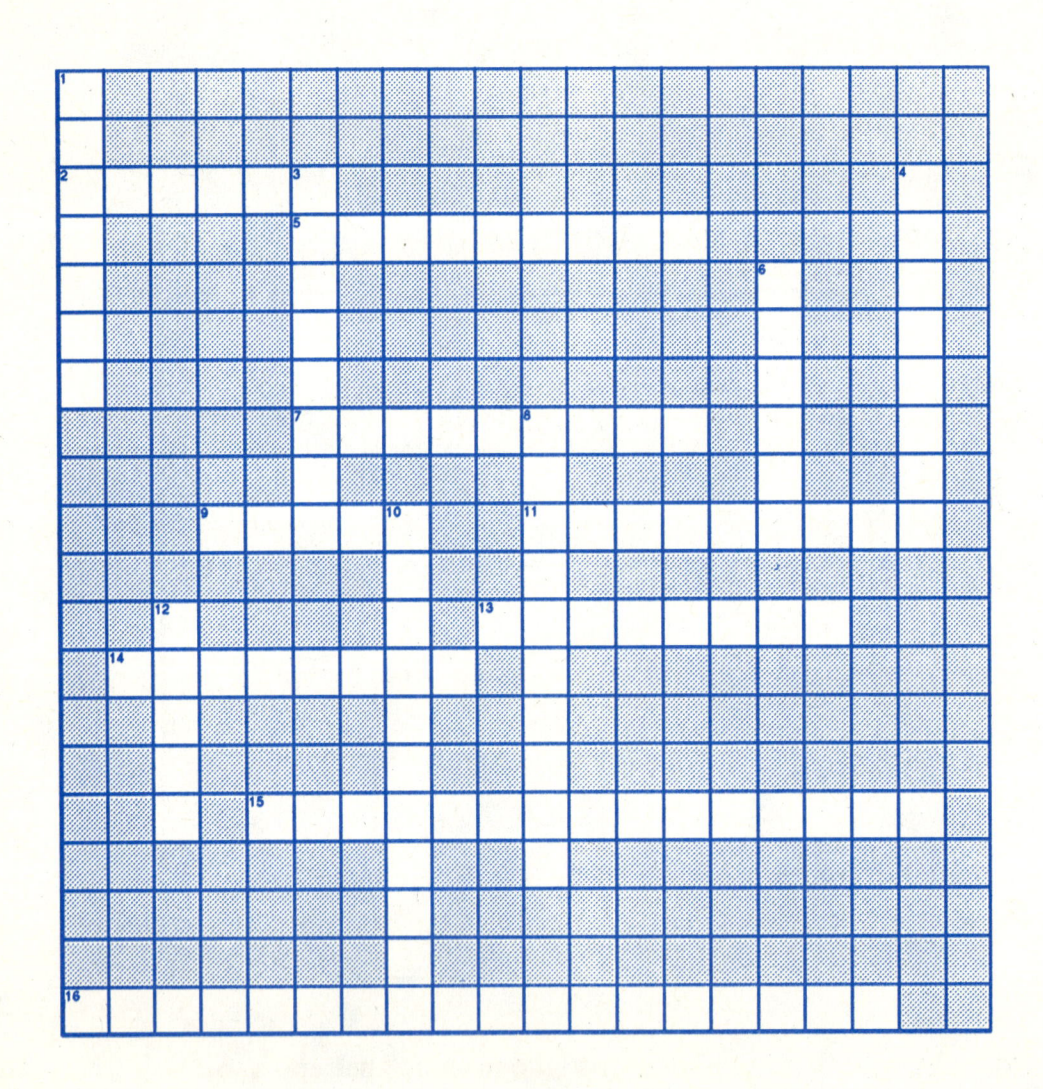

CHAPTER 6

Computer Graphics and Graphs

COMPLETION QUESTIONS

1. Graphics software is any software that is capable of producing _____.
2. Software that makes graphs is known as _____ software.
3. Graphs or charts show data in the form of _____.
4. Each dot on the computer screen is called a _____.
5. Each dot on the screen can be set to the desired color by using a _____ program.
6. Paint programs are typically operated by making choices from _____.
7. Various icons such as a pencil, brush, paint bucket, or eraser, which are chosen to work on a drawing, are known as _____.
8. The _____ or _____ tool is used for freeform drawing.
9. To draw circles or boxes, you use tools such as the _____ or _____.
10. To clean up a drawing you would probably use the _____ tool.
11. To fill in areas with color, you would use the _____ tool.
12. Software that can make pictures move is known as _____ software.
13. To design more detailed objects that will be manufactured _____ software can be used.
14. CAD software stores images as _____ formulas.
15. Graphing programs are driven by _____ that shows the numbers to be graphed.

16. To compare several values, you would probably use a _____ or _____ graph.

17. To show how data is divided into its parts, you would use a _____ chart.

18. To show changes in data over time, a _____ graph would be most appropriate.

19. Data to be charted might be entered into rows and columns in a _____.

20. While some graphing programs take data from a spreadsheet, others take it from a _____ or directly from the computer screen.

IDENTIFICATION QUESTIONS

Below you will find a drawing produced with the help of a paint program. Lettered callouts point to various places in the painting. On each corresponding answer line, write the name of the tool that you think was used to create that part of the drawing. Explain why you answered each of the questions the way you did.

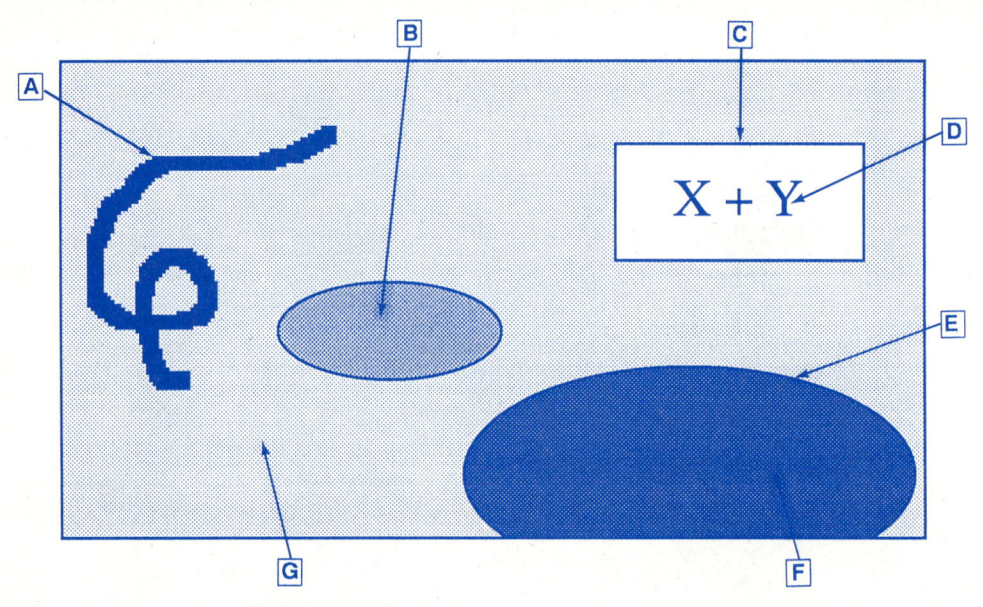

A _____
B _____
C _____
D _____
E _____
F _____
G _____

Name _____ Class _____ Date _____

WORKING AT THE COMPUTER

Complete the following projects. You will need the *Computer Confidence* Template Disk to complete the projects that are marked with a diskette icon.

1. In the spaces provided, manually draw each of the graphs indicated below. If computer software is available, use it to graph the same data. Compare the manual graph and the computer graph.

    a. On the reading portion of a standardized test, Mrs. Groom's class averaged a percentile score of 60, Mr. Sakavoy's averaged 80, and Mrs. Maxie's averaged 70. Draw a column graph showing these scores.

    b. In the vote for class president, Dale received 30%, Marsha received 20%, and Boris received the remainder. Draw a pie chart showing the election results.

c. On three successive tests, Wyler scores 70, 90, and 80. On the same three tests, Eubanks scored 75, 80, and 90. Draw a line graph showing the scores for these two students. Use a legend on the graph.

2. Pretend that you are a computer columnist and help consultant for the school newspaper. As a standard part of your column, you invite students to write to you with questions for which you will write individual answers. To help you write these answers more easily, you have stored on disk a collection of standard paragraphs from which you may select. Those files are on the template disk in Files C6A4A through C6A4F. Here is a brief description of what is in each file:

C6A4A	Definition of a Graphics Program
C6A4B	Definition of a Graphing Program
C6A4C	Definition of a Paint Program
C6A4D	Definition of a Draw Program
C6A4E	Definition of a CAD Program
C6A4F	Kinds of Graphs

Two letters you have received from fellow students are provided in Figure 6.1 and 6.2. For each of them, select the best paragraphs that help answer the question. (You may find it helpful to first load and print each file so that you can see exactly what information is included in the file.) Assemble the paragraphs needed for each letter. (Some word processing programs use a "merge" command to do this.) You may also need to add or change the text of the standard paragraphs to complete a good answer. For example, you will need to provide a salutation and introductory sentence or two for each response, as well as a closing sentence. Include your name as part of the closing for each letter.

Save your response to the first letter as C6A4XXX1 (replacing XXX with your initials), and then print the response. After your response to the first letter has been prepared, complete a response to the second letter. Save this response as C6A4XXX2 and print the response.

Name _____ Class _____ Date _____

Dear Consultant:

I am trying to decide which of two programs to buy. The box for the first program describes it as a pixel painting program. The other is described as a drawing program whose images can easily be resized and moved. I don't understand the difference between the two programs. Can you help?

Sincerely,

Confused

Figure 6.1

The first student who needs your advice would like to know the difference between a pixel paint program and a drawing program.

Dear Consultant:

A friend of mine used a computer program to create graphs and charts to include in her science project. What kind of program can I use to create graphs and charts? What are the different kinds of graphs and charts? Help!

Sincerely,

Trying for an "A" in Science

Figure 6.2

Can you help this student by describing some of the graphing software you've learned about?

MicroTools Instructions:

a. Load the *MicroTools* software and select Option 1 (Word Processing option).

b. Press <Command><F> to begin the File Operations command. Press <L> to select the load option. Highlight **C6A4A** and press <Enter/Return> to load the file.

c. If a printer is attached to your computer, press <Command><P> to begin the Print command. (If a printer is not available, just read the paragraph on the screen). Press <P> for printer and <F> for formatted. Press

Chapter 6 ♦ Computer Graphics and Graphs   45

<Enter/Return> twice to indicate start printing at the first page and continue through the last page.

d. Repeat Steps b and c for files C6A4B, C6A4C, C6A4D, C6A4E, and C6A4F. When you have printed or read all of the paragraphs, press <Command><E> to erase the document currently displayed from your screen. If you are asked if you want to save the text in memory first, press <N>.

e. Review each of the paragraphs and decide which paragraphs should be used to respond to the first letter. Begin the letter with a salutation and then key an introductory sentence or two. Then use the Merge option of the File Operations command to merge the necessary files from the template disk into your document. For example, if you decided that the paragraph included in file C6A4A would be important to include as part of your answer, you would follow these steps to merge the file into your document:

- Move your cursor to the point in your document at which you want the merged file to be inserted.
- Press <Command><F> to begin the File Operations command.
- Press <M> to select the Merge option.
- Highlight the file you wish to merge (for this example, you would highlight C6A4A) and press <Enter/Return>. The file will be merged into your existing document.

When you have merged all of the paragraphs you wish to use, review them and add any additional text that you think would be helpful. Key a closing sentence or two. When you key the closing to the letter, use your name or "Computer Consultant" as the sender. Proofread your document and correct any errors you find.

Save your response as C6A4XXX1 (replacing XXX with your initials). Use the Print command (<Command><P>) to print your document. (Refer to Step c if you need assistance printing the document.) When the document has been printed, press <Command><E> to erase the word processing screen.

f. Follow the instructions in Step e to prepare a response to the second letter. This time, save your document as C6A4XXX2.

g. Press <Command><Q> to quit the word processing program.

h. Press <Esc> to exit *MicroTools*.

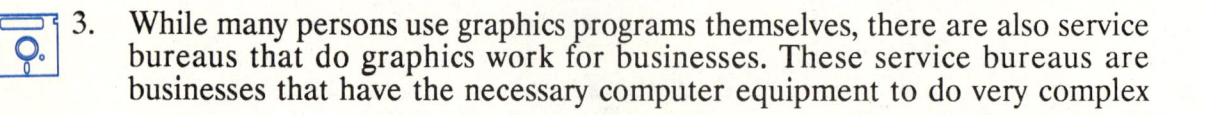

3. While many persons use graphics programs themselves, there are also service bureaus that do graphics work for businesses. These service bureaus are businesses that have the necessary computer equipment to do very complex

Name _____ Class _____ Date _____

graphics work. They sell their services to businesses that do not have the equipment, time, or expertise to do graphics work themselves.

For this activity, pretend that you work for a graphic service bureau. Your company uses a spreadsheet to prepare bills for your customers. To do this, you have a standard spreadsheet already set up with the rates you charge for various services. This spreadsheet is stored on the template disk under the name C6A5 and is shown in Figure 6.3.

```
            A              B           C         D        E
  1:  GREAT GRAPHICS, LTD.         Completed by:
  2:  415 Leith Lane
  3:  Fayetteville, GA 30214-2582
  4:
  5:  Project Billing--Proj. #:
  6:
  7:             Customer Name:
  8:                    Street:
  9:          City, State, ZIP:
 10:
 11:  Explanation of Charges          Rate    Hours   Amount
 12:  ----------------------          ----    -----   ------
 13:  Planning and Review             48.00            0.00
 14:  Graphic Artist                  36.00            0.00
 15:  Graphing Technician             28.00            0.00
 16:  Page Layout                     36.00            0.00
 17:  Final Output Media              -----   ----     0.00
 18:
 19:             Total                                 0.00
 20:                                                 ========
```

Figure 6.3
Template File C6A5

To prepare a bill, load your spreadsheet program, and then load File C6A5. Enter your name in Cell E1. Move your cursor to Cell C5 and enter the project number. Enter the customer's name, street, and city, state, and ZIP code in Cells C7, C8, and C9. Enter the hours spent on each activity in the appropriate cells in Column D. The "Final Output Media" charge should be entered in Cell E17 as a dollar amount. The spreadsheet will automatically calculate how much the customer owes.

To complete your work for this activity, prepare bills for the three projects for which information is provided below in Table 6.1. After each bill has been prepared, save the file using the filename provided (adding XXX with your initials), and then print a copy of the spreadsheet. To prepare the next bill, load File C6A5 and begin the process again.

Chapter 6 ♦ Computer Graphics and Graphs

Project Number:	PN91321
Name:	Farley Fairings Corporation
Address:	313 Wright Way, Muskegon, OK 89872-3528
Planning & Reviewing:	1.5 hours
Graphic Artist:	9.2 hours
Graphing Technician:	.1 hour
Page Layout:	3.5 hours
Final Output Media:	$124.00

Save as C6A5XXX1

Project Number:	PN91322
Name:	Albecorn Industries
Address:	3 Albecorn Way, Thomasville, GA 31792-8862
Planning & Reviewing:	.5 hours
Graphic Artist:	
Graphing Technician:	1 hour
Page Layout:	
Final Output Media:	$18.00

Save as C6A5XXX2

Project Number:	PN91323
Name:	Zambruski & Larson Consulting
Address:	614 Southmont, Cambridge, MA 10232-3443
Planning & Reviewing:	5 hours
Graphic Artist:	28.5 hours
Graphing Technician:	
Page Layout:	
Final Output Media:	$48.00

Save as C6A5XXX3

Table 6.1
Project Information

MicroTools Instructions:

a. Load the *MicroTools* software and select Option 2, the Spreadsheet option.

b. For each of the three projects, complete the following:

1. Press <Command><F> to begin the File Operations command. Press <L> to select the Load option. Highlight File **C6A5** and press <Enter/Return>.

2. Move the cursor to Cell E1 and enter your name.

3. Move the cursor to Cell C5 and enter the project number for the project.

4. Move the cursor to Cell C7 and enter the customer's name. In Cell C8, enter the customer's street address. Since the street address begins with a number, key an apostrophe (') before the street number. This will tell *MicroTools* that the address will contain letters and

Name _____ Class _____ Date _____

numbers and cannot be used in mathematical calculations. In Cell C9, enter the customer's city, state, and ZIP code.

5. Beginning in Cell D13, enter the hours for each of the items indicated. Notice that the amount is automatically totalled for you. When you reach the Final Output Media category, move the cursor to cell E17 and enter the dollar amount provided. (Do not key the dollar sign as part of the dollar amount.)

6. When all of the information has been entered, press <Command><F> to begin the File Operations command. Press <S> to select the Save option. ***DO NOT USE THE EXISTING FILENAME OF C6A5 WHEN YOU SAVE THE FILE!*** Instead, use the name provided for each project.

7. Press <Command><P> to begin the Print command. Press <P> to print the spreadsheet to a printer. Press <P> again to print the spreadsheet as is.

c. When all of the spreadsheets have been prepared, press <Command><Q> to quit the spreadsheet program.

d. Press <Esc> to exit *MicroTools*.

Chapter 6 ♦ Computer Graphics and Graphs

CROSSWORD PUZZLE

Complete the following Crossword Puzzle. All answers to the puzzle can be found in Chapter 6 of your textbook.

Across Clues
1. used in a paint program to make freeform lines
4. used to fill in areas with color
6. type of program that can produce pictures
8. type of graph with horizontal lines of varying lengths
10. a good kind of graph for showing changes in data over time
12. a kind of program that uses the computer display as a canvas
13. a good kind of chart for showing the division of data into parts
14. kind of graphics program used to design things
15. tool used for drawing boxes

Down Clues
2. tool used for cutting a part of a painting
3. tool used to remove lines
5. one possible source of data for a graphing program
6. a type of program that draws charts representing data
7. a type of graph that uses vertical bars to represent data
9. the process of making pictures move
11. the tool used for drawing circles and ovals

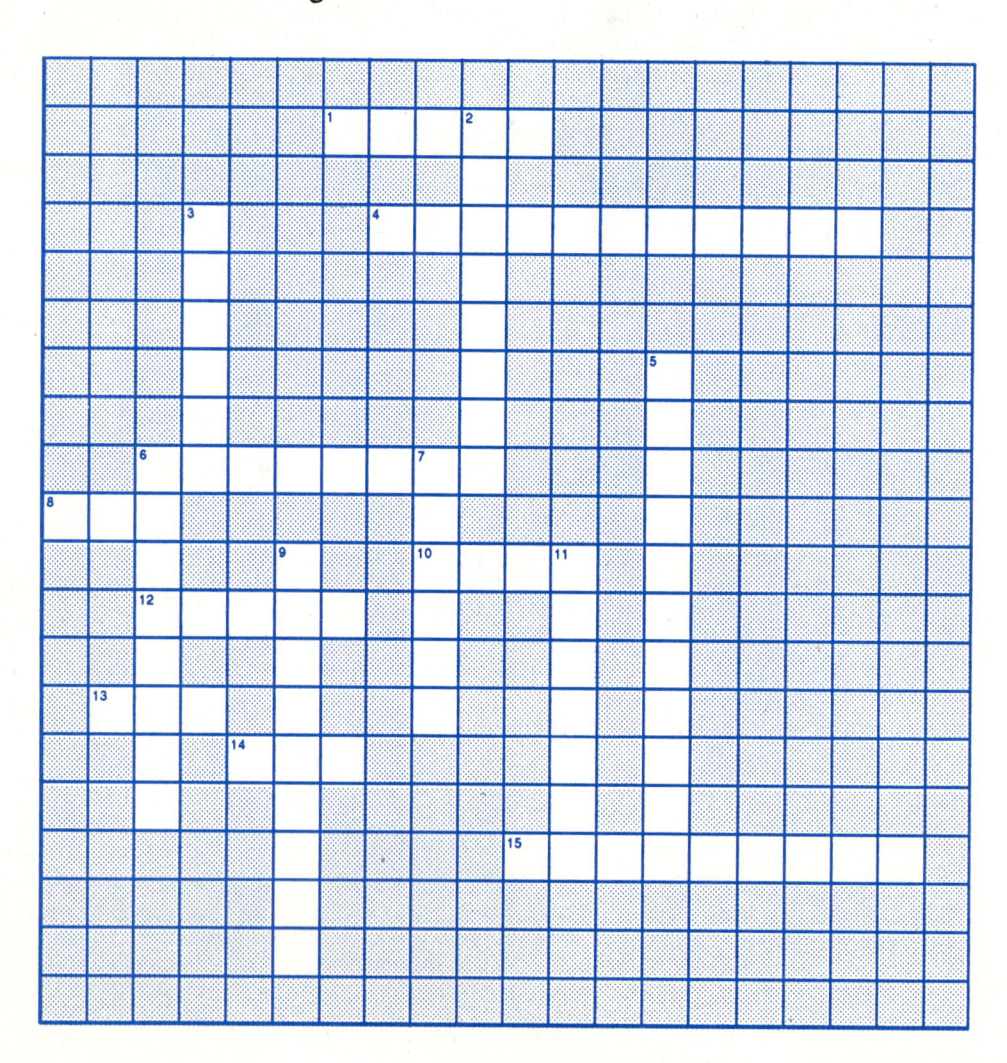

Name _____ Class _____ Date _____

CHAPTER 7

Computer Communication

COMPLETION QUESTIONS

1. Computers need to communicate so that they can get _____ from other computers or give _____ to other computers.

2. The ability of one computer to talk to another is known as _____.

3. The computer can keep you updated on things such as world events, _____, and _____ of your favorite teams.

4. In addition to giving you a flight schedule, the use of your computer connected to an airline reservation system can tell you how frequently _____.

5. Merchandise or _____ of just about any kind can be purchased by computer.

6. School principals, _____, or _____ can use the computer to do research.

7. In the computer, electricity is either on or off, or made _____ or _____.

8. A binary digit may be referred to by its short name of _____.

9. A byte is made up of _____ bits.

10. A _____ represents one character.

11. Using eight bits to represent each character, a total of _____ different characters can be represented.

51

12. The code used to code characters on most microcomputers is known as _____, which is short for _____ _____.

13. Characters that tell how data is to be transmitted or formatted are known as _____.

14. When using ASCII, code numbers from _____ through _____ are fairly standard, while those from _____ through _____ may be used differently by different manufacturers.

15. A code used by many larger computers is _____, which is short for _____.

16. A group of computers located close to each other and connected to communicate with each other is known as a _____ or _____.

17. Connecting computers allows the sharing of data, the sharing of peripherals such as _____, or sending of electronic _____ from one user to another.

18. When computers that need to communicate with each other are not located close to each other, _____ may be used to connect them to telephone lines.

19. The use of an ISDN phone line eliminates the need for a _____.

20. Companies that use large computers to supply all kinds of data and services to users whose computers call the large computer are known as _____.

21. Using a computer _____, users are able to post and read messages.

22. Information utilities and bulletin boards are usually open to the public, but most large businesses use some kind of _____ for private use.

MATCHING EXERCISES

Match the following terms with the clues shown on the next page. Write the letter of each term on the appropriate line.

A. modem
B. ASCII
C. control character
D. bit
E. ISDN
F. byte
G. computer communications
H. local area network

Name _____ Class _____ Date _____

1. _____ It's a code, but it's not secret.
2. _____ You can find it in a computer or a horse's mouth.
3. _____ You can take one from an apple or store a character in it.
4. _____ When two computers talk, it's called ____ ____.
5. _____ It's a real character but you can't see it.
6. _____ It can put the modem in the unemployment line.
7. _____ It likes to be close.
8. _____ It talks on the phone but knows no words.

CODING AND DECODING

1. Write in the ASCII code numbers that would be used to represent each letter in the following messages.

    a. ___ ___ ___ ___ ___ ___
       H   E   L   L   O   !

    b. ___ ___ ___ ___ ___ ___ ___ ___ ___
       C   o   d   e   s   a   r   e

       ___ ___ ___
       f   u   n

    c. ___ ___ ___ ___ ___ ___ ___ ___ ___
       (Your first name)

2. Write in the messages represented by the following ASCII codes.

    a. ___ ___ ___
       070 085 078

    b. ___ ___ ___ ___ ___ ___ ___ ___ ___ ___
       089 111 117 032 107 110 111 119 032 097

       ___ ___ ___ ___ ___ ___ ___
       032 083 069 067 082 069 084

    c. ___ ___ ___ ___ ___ ___ ___ ___
       032 084 104 101 032 069 110 100

WORKING AT THE COMPUTER

Complete the following projects. You will need the *Computer Confidence Template Disk* to complete the projects that are marked with a diskette icon.

1. You learned about the importance of ASCII codes in Chapter 7 of your textbook. In this project, you will use a database that has been created for you, File C7A1. Each record in the database file consists of the following two fields: ASCII CODE and CHARACTER. In this project, you will search the database to find ASCII codes for messages you create.

Chapter 7 ♦ Computer Communication

Begin this project by writing in the space provided in Table 7.1 the following items: the name of your favorite fruit; your first and last names; and the name of your school. Do not exceed 18 characters for any one message. If one of your messages is longer than 18 characters, think of a way to make it shorter. Search the database for each letter, and write the corresponding ASCII code to the right of the letter. For example, if your favorite fruit is kumquat, your paper will look like this:

FAVORITE FRUIT

LETTER	ASCII
k	107
u	117
m	109
q	113
u	117
a	097
t	116

When you have searched for all of the necessary information, exit your database program.

FAVORITE FRUIT		FIRST & LAST NAME		SCHOOL NAME	
LETTER	ASCII	LETTER	ASCII	LETTER	ASCII
___	___	___	___	___	___
___	___	___	___	___	___
___	___	___	___	___	___
___	___	___	___	___	___
___	___	___	___	___	___
___	___	___	___	___	___
___	___	___	___	___	___
___	___	___	___	___	___
___	___	___	___	___	___
___	___	___	___	___	___
___	___	___	___	___	___
___	___	___	___	___	___
___	___	___	___	___	___
___	___	___	___	___	___
___	___	___	___	___	___
___	___	___	___	___	___
___	___	___	___	___	___
___	___	___	___	___	___

Table 7.1

The database can help you translate alphabetic characters to ASCII code.

Name _____ Class _____ Date _____

> *MicroTools* Instructions:
>
> a. Fill in only the letters requested in Table 7.1.
>
> b. Load your *MicroTools* software. Select Option 3, the Database option.
>
> c. Press <L> to load an existing database. Highlight File **C7A1** and press <Enter/Return>.
>
> d. Press <Command><S> to begin the search command. You will be prompted to select the type of search you wish to perform. Press <E> for Equal to.
>
> e. You will be asked to enter the number of the field to be searched. Enter <2> as the field to be searched.
>
> f. You will be asked to enter the value for be searched for in the CHARACTER field (Field 2). Enter the first letter for which you wish to search. For example, if you favorite fruit is kumquat, enter "K" as the letter for which to search.
>
> g. You will be given the opportunity to search for information in another field. Enter <D> for Done.
>
> h. When the database searches for the character you entered, the program does not distinguish between uppercase and lowercase characters. If you entered a lowercase character, such as "a," the program will find "A" first. To continue the search, press <Command> <N> to display the next record that meets your search criteria. By looking at the record, you can find the ASCII code for that letter. Write the ASCII code in the appropriate space in Table 7.1.
>
> i. Repeat Steps d-h until you have found the ASCII codes for all of the letters in each of your messages.
>
> j. Press <Command><Q> to quit the database program. If you are asked if you wish to save the database, press <N>.
>
> k. Press <Esc> to exit *MicroTools*.

2. On your template disk is a spreadsheet file named C7A2. You will use it to help convert messages into the binary codes that are communicated by the computer. Make sure you complete Project 1 before attempting Project 2. The spreadsheet is shown on the next page.

Chapter 7 ♦ Computer Communication

	A	B	C	D	E	F	G	H	I	J	K
1:	Letter	ASCII	128	64	32	16	8	4	2	1	Check
2:	======	=====	===	===	===	===	===	===	===	===	=====
3:											0
4:											0
5:											0
6:											0
7:											0
8:											0
9:											0
10:											0
11:											0
12:											0
13:											0
14:											0
15:											0
16:											0
17:											0
18:											0
19:											0
20:											0
21:											
22:											
23:											
24:											

You will key whatever message you desire, as long as the message is not larger than 18 characters (including spaces). For example, if your name was Kelly Lufkin, your spreadsheet would look like the one shown below.

	A	B	C	D	E	F	G	H	I	J	K
1:	Letter	ASCII	128	64	32	16	8	4	2	1	Check
2:	======	=====	===	===	===	===	===	===	===	===	=====
3:	K	75	0	1	0	0	1	0	1	1	75
4:	e	101	0	1	1	0	0	1	0	1	101
5:	l	108	0	1	1	0	1	1	0	0	108
6:	l	108	0	1	1	0	1	1	0	0	108
7:	y	121	0	1	1	1	1	0	0	1	121
8:		32	0	0	1	0	0	0	0	0	32
9:	L	76	0	1	0	0	1	1	0	0	76
10:	u	117	0	1	1	1	0	1	0	1	117
11:	f	102	0	1	1	0	0	1	1	0	102
12:	k	107	0	1	1	0	1	0	1	1	107
13:	i	105	0	1	1	0	1	0	0	1	105
14:	n	110	0	1	1	0	1	1	1	0	110
15:											0
16:											0
17:											0
18:											0
19:											0
20:											0

Name _____ Class _____ Date _____

Do at least the following three messages. Print a copy of the spreadsheet after entering each one.

The name of your favorite fruit
Your first and last names
The name of your school

Load the spreadsheet (C7A2) from disk. In Column A, enter the letters of the desired message. In Column B, enter the ASCII code number you looked up in Project 1. In Columns C through J, enter the ones and zeros necessary to represent the ASCII code. As you enter these ones and zeros, note that the value in Column K changes to show the actual code you have entered to that point. When you finish entering the ones and zeros, the check value in Column K should match the ASCII code in Column B.

MicroTools Instructions:

a. Load your *MicroTools* software. Select Option 2, the Spreadsheet option.

b. Press <Command><F> to begin the File Operations command. Press <L> to select the Load option. Highlight File **C7A2** and press <Enter/Return> to load the file.

c. Key the name of your favorite fruit in Column A. Make sure to key each letter in a different row.

d. In Column B, key the ASCII code for each of the letters entered in Column A. You can find the ASCII code numbers you looked up in Project 1.

e. In Columns C through J, enter the ones and zeros necessary to represent the ASCII code. As you enter these ones and zeros, note that the value you have entered to that point. When you finish entering the ones and zeros, the check value in Column K should match the ASCII code in Column B.

f. Press <Command><P> to print the spreadsheet. Press <P> to print the spreadsheet to a printer. Press <P> again to print the spreadsheet.

g. Repeat Steps b-f, this time keying the codes for your first and last names. When you use the File Operations command to load File C7A2, you will be asked if you wish to save the spreadsheet in memory first. Press <N> to tell *MicroTools* that you do not wish to save the spreadsheet.

h. Repeat Steps b-f again, this time keying the codes for the name of your school. If you are asked if you wish to save the spreadsheet in memory first, press <N>.

i. Press <Command><Q> to quit the spreadsheet program. Press <N> if you are asked if you wish to save the spreadsheet in memory first.

j. Press <Esc> to exit *MicroTools*.

Name _____ Class _____ Date _____

CROSSWORD PUZZLE

Using the clues provided, complete the crossword puzzle. Some answers may require more than one word. When that is the case, do not space between words.

Across Clues
2. device that hooks a computer to the phone line
5. the code used on microcomputers
7. eight ones and zeros
8. messages sent from one computer to another
9. the code used by many larger computers
11. network communication over a great distance
13. phone lines of ISDN work with these instead of sounds

Down Clues
1. a group of computers that are located close to each other and are connected to communicate
3. a kind of phone line that does not require the use of a modem to connect a computer
4. a one or zero
6. the kind of character represented by ASCII codes of 1-31
10. can link together computers that are far away from each other
12. the basis on which regular telephone lines work

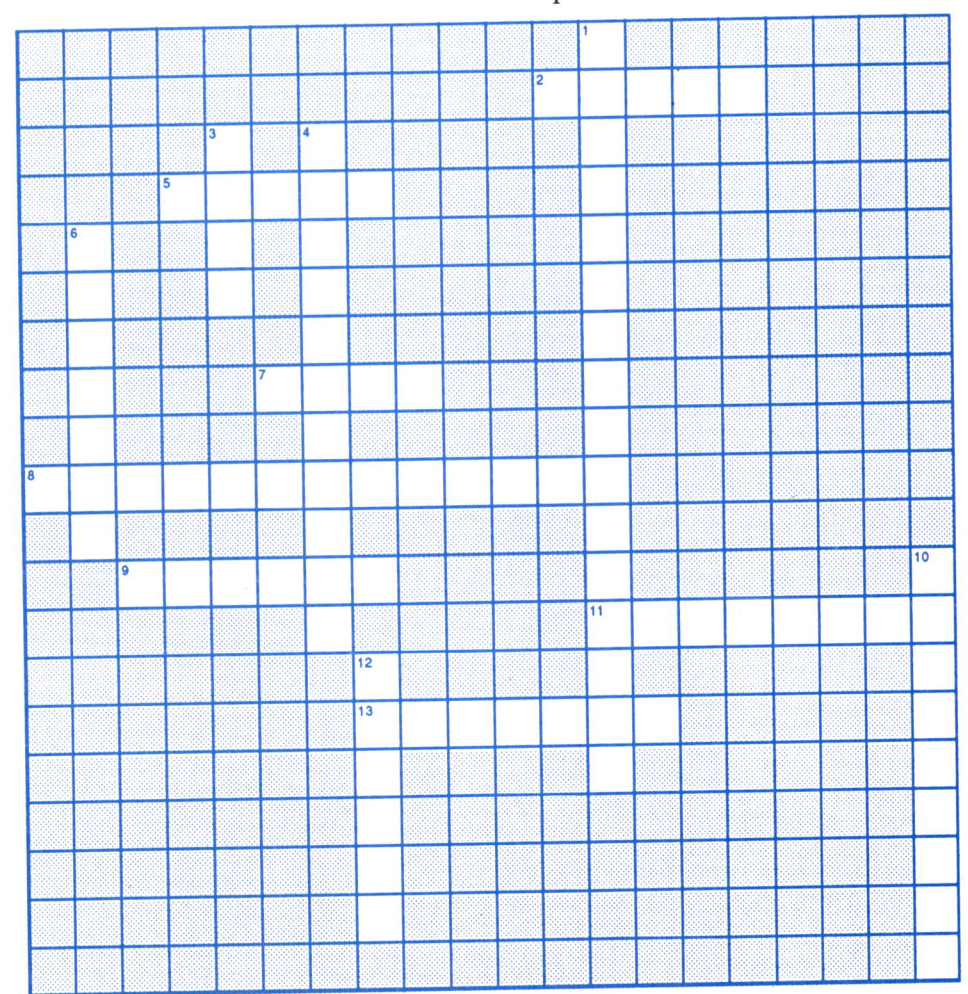

Chapter 7 ♦ Computer Communication

Name _____ Class _____ Date _____

CHAPTER 8

Software Integration

COMPLETION QUESTIONS

1. Integration means a _____ of things.
2. A group of several different kinds of software that work together is known as _____.
3. One of the most commonly used types of integrated software combines _____ and _____.
4. One way to get integrated software is to buy a package in which the _____ is already done.
5. Separate programs that know how to _____ can be integrated.
6. A limited _____ ability is often added to the common combination of spreadsheet and graphing software.
7. *Lotus 1-2-3* popularized the combination of _____, _____, and _____ modules (parts).
8. When the capability of printing pictures is added to word processing programs, _____ ability has been added.
9. When a word processing program shows you on the screen how the page with graphics will look when it is printed, it is said to have _____ capability.
10. Even word processing programs with graphics printing ability cannot yet be used to create _____ pictures.

61

11. Integrated packages that try to provide all the computing power a user needs include functions for _____, _____, _____, _____, and _____.

12. Most inexpensive integrated packages consist of different program modules (parts) that can be reached from the same _____ and have a similar _____.

13. The kinds of programs most likely to suffer from the increasing power of publishing programs are _____ and _____ programs.

14. A common user interface means that _____ is similar in all the modules or packages.

15. A common data format makes it easier for the parts of an integrated package to share _____.

16. An area of memory that is used to hold data from one program module until it is transferred to another module is the _____.

17. A _____ is one of the advantages provided by platforms such as that of *Apple Macintosh* or *Microsoft Windows*.

IDENTIFICATION QUESTIONS

1. Pretend that your school publishes a newsletter for parents. It sometimes includes pictures and diagrams. What kind of integrated software could be used to produce the newsletter?

   _____
   _____
   _____

2. The principal of your school wants to keep records of the grades earned by students from year to year. The principal also wants to produce graphs showing changes in grades from year to year. What kind of integrated software should the principal use?

   _____
   _____
   _____

3. Your teacher wants software to use to prepare handouts for students, to record students' grades, and to call the school's computer from home to work with students' records. What kind of integrated package should your teacher use?

   _____
   _____
   _____

Name _____ Class _____ Date _____

WORKING AT THE COMPUTER

Complete the following projects. You will need the *Computer Confidence* Template Disk to complete the projects that are marked with a diskette icon.

1. For this computer activity, you will use two files from the template disk. These two files are named C8A1WP and C8A1SS. File C8A1WP contains the text of a letter. File C8A1SS contains a spreadsheet. You will print the letter with the spreadsheet's contents included in the letter. First, load and examine the spreadsheet. You will note that it is a listing of best selling toys. Take any steps necessary to ensure that the body of the spreadsheet can be moved into the letter when the letter is printed. Then load the letter and locate the point where the spreadsheet should appear. Delete the line that reads "INSERT SPREADSHEET HERE." Replace "(Your Name)" with your name. Insert the spreadsheet into the text. Save your finished word processing file as C8A1XXX (remember to replace "XXX" with your initials) and print the letter.

   MicroTools Instructions:

   a. Load *MicroTools* and select the spreadsheet option.

   b. Press <Command><F> to begin the File Operations command. Press <L> to load a file. Highlight file C8A1SS and press <Enter/Return>.

   c. Print the spreadsheet to disk without the row and column headings:

      1. Press <Command><P> to print the spreadsheet. Press <F> to print it to a file.
      2. You will be prompted to enter a print file name. Key the name **C8A1SS** as the filename to be created and press <Enter/Return>.
      3. When asked whether to print as is or set special options, press <S> to set special options.
      4. When asked whether to print with row and column headings, press <N>.
      5. When asked whether to print formulas or values, press <V> to print values.
      6. When asked for the upper-left and lower-right cells to be printed, press <Enter/Return> each time to accept the active region.
      7. When asked whether to use standard or wide printer settings, press <S> (standard). If you are prompted to key any special printer codes, simply press <Enter/Return> and the spreadsheet will be printed to disk.

   d. Press <Command><Q> to quit the spreadsheet program and return to the Main Menu.

   e. Select Option 1, Word Processor.

Chapter 8 ♦ Software Integration

f. Press <Command><F> to begin the File Operations command. Press <L> to load a file. Highlight file C8A1WP and press <Enter/Return>.

g. Move your cursor to Line 23 (the line that reads INSERT SPREADSHEET HERE). Press <Command><D> to delete the line.

h. Press <Command><F> to begin the File Operations command. Press <M> to select the Merge option. Highlight file C8A1SS and press <Enter/Return>.

i. Move your cursor to the last line of the document. Press <Command><O> to switch to Overstrike mode and key your name. If you have a short name, you may need to add a few spaces after your name to completely cover the existing text.

j. Save the letter as C8A1XXX (remember to replace "XXX" with your initials).

k. Press <Command><P> to begin the Print command. Press <P> to print the letter to the printer. Press <F> to print a formatted version of the letter. Press <Enter/Return> two times to print the entire letter.

l. Press <Command><Q> to quit the word processor.

m. Press <Esc> to exit *MicroTools*.

CROSSWORD PUZZLE

Complete the following Crossword Puzzle. All answers to the puzzle can be found in Chapter 8 of your textbook.

Across Clues
1. used to enter text for processing by a publishing program
5. one of the advantages integrated software has over separate programs
8. "put together"
10. a kind of software that is frequently paired with spreadsheets
11. a common one of these makes learning and using programs easier
12. using the same one of these makes it easier for modules to share data

Down Clues
2. frequently combined with spreadsheet and graphing abilities
3. frequently paired with word processing or publishing programs
4. frequently matched with word processing and graphics
6. an area of memory that holds data that is to be copied from one area to another
7. frequently used to enter data that is to be graphed
9. a common one of these makes it easier to share data

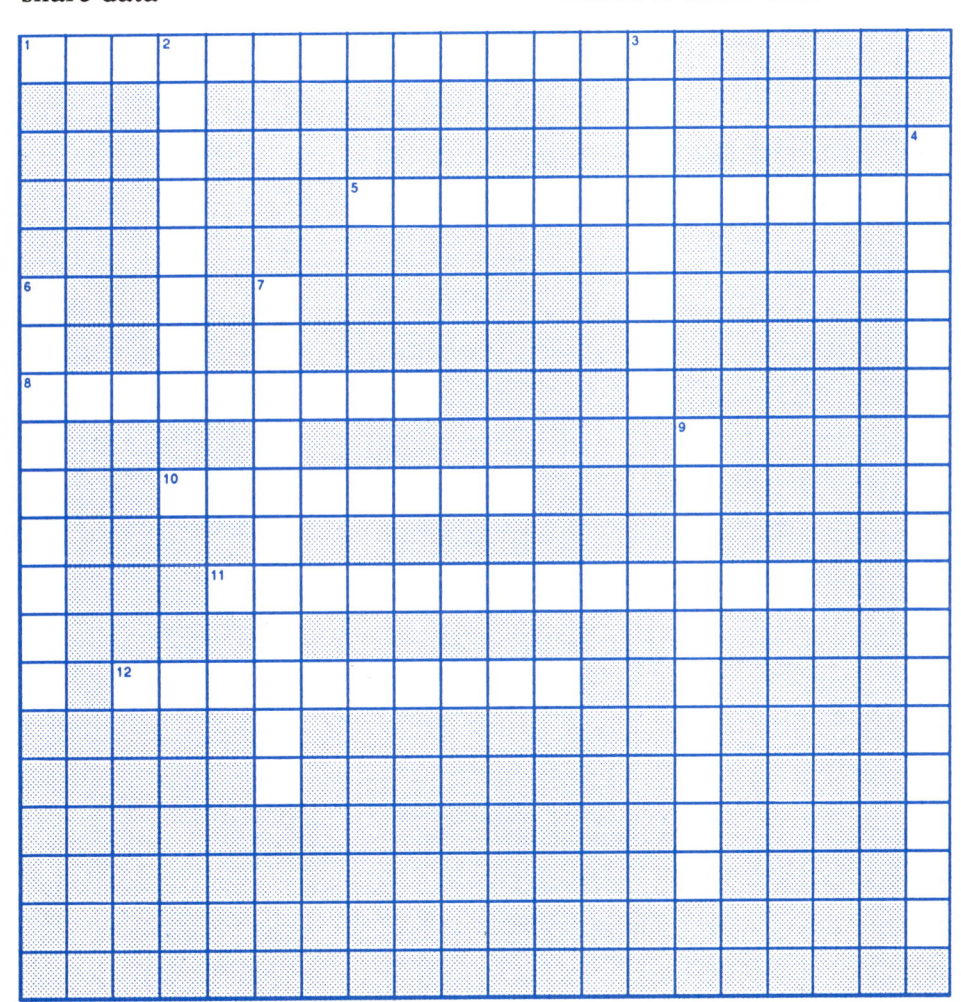

CHAPTER 9

System Software

COMPLETION QUESTIONS

1. The software that controls the operation of the computer is known as the _____.

2. The _____, _____, and _____ are controlled by the operating system of a computer.

3. The two areas into which operating system functions can be categorized are _____ and _____ the performance of the parts of the system.

4. All operating systems control the _____.

5. The entire operating system of a computer can be stored in _____.

6. The control of the hardware by the operating system begins when _____.

7. Application programs can ask the operating system to do such things as _____ files onto or from a disk.

8. A problem that does not cause a program to stop running is known as a _____ error.

9. Some operating systems can keep up with the number of attempted _____ by dishonest people or with the length of _____ that the computer takes to respond.

10. All computer work uses the three steps of _____, _____, and _____.
11. During the _____ step, data is brought into the computer from a device such as a disk drive or keyboard.
12. During the _____ step, the results of processing are communicated.
13. Computations are accomplished during the _____ step.
14. An operating system that can run only one program at a time is known as a _____ operating system.
15. Multitasking operating systems are not suitable for use on _____ microcomputers.
16. An operating system that can run more than one program at once is known as a _____ operating system.
17. An operating system that can handle several users at once is known as a _____ operating system.
18. The operating system usually used with Apple II computers is either _____ or _____.
19. The operating system usually used with inexpensive IBM or compatible computers is _____ or _____.
20. The method used to communicate with the operating system is known as the _____.
21. To provide a menu for a command-driven operating system, a person may use an _____.
22. Operating system commands that are loaded from disk as needed are called _____ commands or _____.
23. Utility programs usually do _____ chores.
24. Different operating systems usually store _____ on disks in different ways.
25. In general, more powerful operating systems require more powerful _____ on which to run.

MATCHING EXERCISES

Match the following terms with the clues on the next page. Write the letter of each term on the appropriate line.

A. operating system
B. read only memory (ROM)
C. single-program execution operating system
D. multitasking operating system
E. time-share operating system
F. user interface
G. operating system shell
H. utility

Name _____ Class _____ Date _____

1. _____ It has a "one track mind."
2. _____ You won't find it in an ocean, but you will find it updating old operating systems.
3. _____ This operating system will work for the group or just for one.
4. _____ It's the "king" software.
5. _____ It's not a maid, but it does the housekeeping.
6. _____ It might make a good cook because it can "serve" a lot of people at once.
7. _____ It's a permanent home for the operating system, not a hotel.
8. _____ It's the language you must speak to the computer.

WORKING AT THE COMPUTER

Complete the following projects. You will need the *Computer Confidence* Template Disk to complete the projects that are marked with a diskette icon.

1. Format a diskette for use with a computer that is available to you. Be sure you use a new disk or one that contains no valuable data; any existing data will be erased when you format the disk. On the line below, write the command or menu choice you use to format the disk.

   _____

2. Using your word processing program, start printing any document of your choice (either one you have entered or one from the template disk). When the document starts printing, try to give the command or make the menu choice to enter a new document. On the lines below write what happens; then indicate whether you saw any evidence that your computer was doing multitasking.

   _____
   _____
   _____
   _____
   _____

3. On the template disk is a document giving general descriptions of several common operating system functions. The document is named C9A3. You will change the document so that it states the exact commands or menu choices used on your system to accomplish the functions.

   Load your word processor, and then load file C9A3. Replace the blank lines with the information requested. For example, replace the blank line next to "Disk, Directory:" with the command used by your computer to display a directory of a disk.

Chapter 9 ♦ System Software

When you have replaced all of the blank lines save your file as C9A3XXX (remember to replace "XXX" with your initials). Print your file, and exit the word processor.

> *MicroTools* Instructions:
>
> a. Load *MicroTools*. Select the Word Processor option. Press <Command><F> to begin the File Operations command. Press <L> and load the document named C9A3.
>
> b. At the places indicated in the document, replace the blank lines with your name, the name of your computer, and the operating system it uses.
>
> c. At the indicated places in the document, key the correct commands or menu choices that you use with your operating system to carry out the functions.
>
> d. Save your document as C9A3XXX. (XXX should be replaced by your initials.)
>
> e. Print a copy of the modified document.
>
> f. Press <Command><Q> to quit the word processor. Press <Esc> to exit *MicroTools*.

CROSSWORD PUZZLE

Complete the Crossword Puzzle contained on this and the next page. All answers to the puzzle can be found in Chapter 9 of your textbook.

Across Clues

1. the program that controls the computer
5. an operating system that can do more than one thing at a time
8. a "housekeeping" program
10. the method used to communicate with an operating system
11. a problem that does not cause a program to stop running
13. operating systems with many capabilities need computers with a lot of this to run

Down Clues

2. a place where the operating systems is sometimes stored
3. an operating system that can handle more than one user at a time
4. an operating system that can run only one program at a time
6. an "add-on" that provides menus for command-driven operating systems
7. an operating system command that must be loaded from disk
9. one of the three steps that computers perform
12. a command used to copy data in case of a power failure or a bad disk

Name _____ Class _____ Date _____

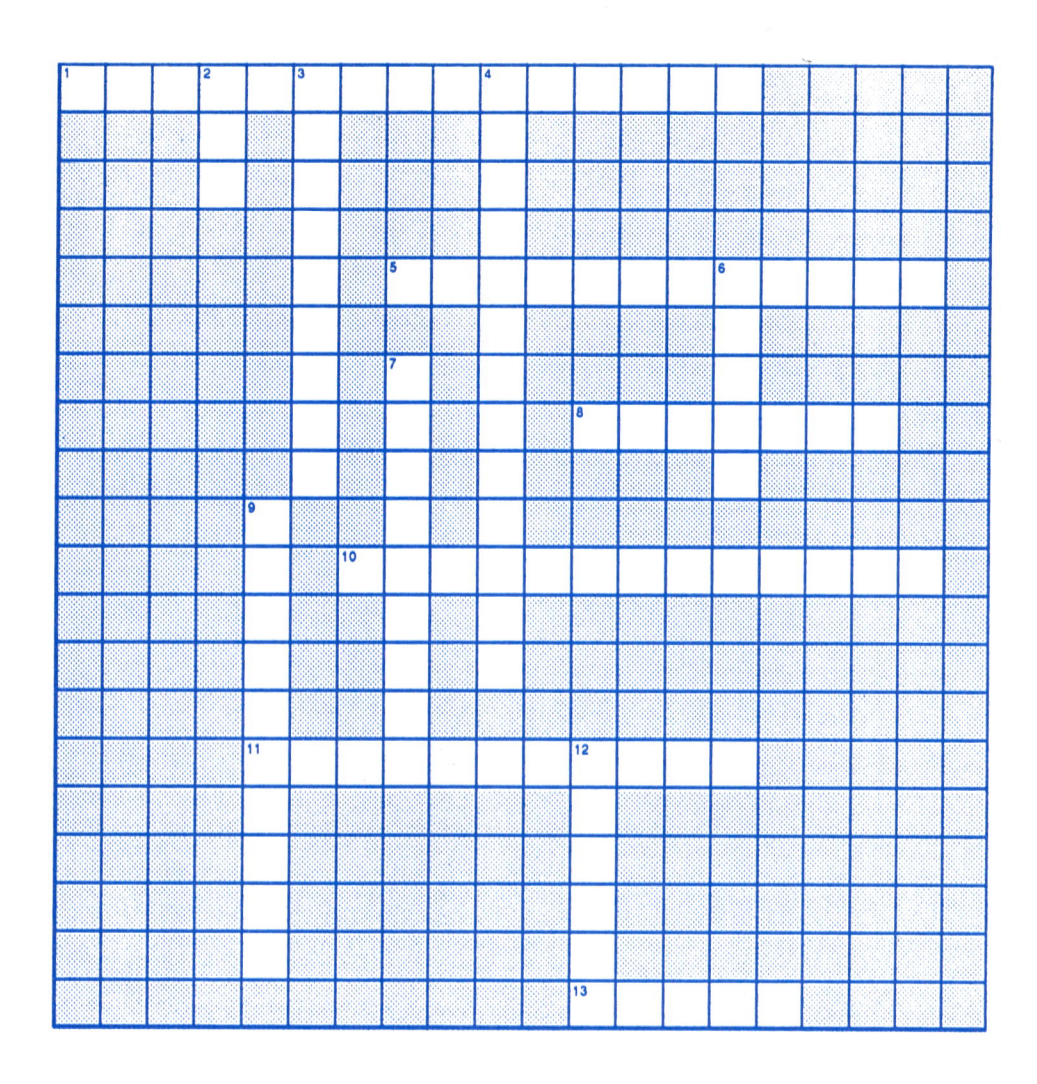

Name _____ Class _____ Date _____

CHAPTER 10

Input Devices and Media

COMPLETION QUESTIONS

1. The putting in or feeding in of data to a computer system is known as _____.

2. An _____ receives data and sends it to the processor.

3. The material that data is recorded on before it is sent to the computer is the _____.

4. The most commonly used input device is the _____.

5. The two basic designs of the typewriter style keyboard are _____ and _____.

6. The keyboard design that is often used to teach children is an _____ design.

7. Some cafeterias use _____ terminals because the programmed keys on it can be used to list each food item that is for sale.

8. The _____ can be used to pay bills and order products.

9. A _____ is used in grocery stores to read bars or lines that are printed on the package of a product.

10. _____ are used to scan printed material and images and store the information in a computer's memory.

11. _____ are used by automatic teller machines to read magnetic tape strips on credit and bank cards.

73

12. _____ equipment scans numbers, letters, and symbols directly from a typed, printed, or handwritten page.

13. _____ equipment senses the presence or absence of marks made by regular pencil or pen on specially designed forms.

14. The controller device that is very common in computerized games and allows cursor movement in all directions is the _____.

15. A _____ is a pointing device that the user moves on a flat surface to move the cursor around the screen.

16. A _____ looks like a normal computer screen, but it can detect a person's touch at the point where a finger touches the screen.

17. A _____ is a pointing device that may be used to point out locations or to draw images on a computer screen.

18. A _____ is used to "hear" the human voice and translate the voice into electronic signals.

19. A _____ is a computerized sensor that sends information to the computer about an event while it is happening.

20. A _____ changes shapes into numbers for storage by computers.

21. A _____ is used to connect electronic musical instruments such as keyboards and rhythm machines to computers.

MATCHING EXERCISES

Match the following terms with their clues. Write the letter of each term on the appropriate line.

A. MIDI
B. bar-code scanner
C. paddle
D. mouse
E. light pen
F. touch-tone telephone
G. real-time sensor
H. point-of-sale terminal
I. magnetic scanner
J. optical-mark recognition

1. _____ moves the cursor horizontally and vertically
2. _____ rolls on a flat surface
3. _____ connects musical instruments to computers
4. _____ draws on the screen
5. _____ has a numeric keyboard which produces sounds that a computer can understand

Name _____ Class _____ Date _____

6. _____ grades tests
7. _____ saves grocery store employees from marking a price on each item
8. _____ scans magnetic tape
9. _____ can sense intruders
10. _____ uses programmed keys to "ring up" sales

WHAT AM I?

In the following exercise, fill in the terms that best match the clues given.

1. I listen for your voice and make the computer do what I am told. What am I?

   _____

2. I roll around on a flat surface and cause the cursor to move around on the screen. Is that a cat chasing me? What am I?

   _____

3. I am used with computerized games and help to move the cursor on the screen, but I can only move the cursor horizontally and vertically. What am I?

   _____

4. I am the keyboard that was developed by Christopher Sholes. What am I?

   _____

5. I pay close attention to the tasks to which I am assigned. I sense when something goes wrong, like an intruder in a house or yard. What am I?

   _____

6. I reach out and touch someone but I don't say a word; I just pay bills and order products with a tone. What am I?

   _____

7. With me you can just point with your finger to the menu item you want to use. What am I?

   _____

8. My name makes me sound like I'm athletic, but all I do is roll around while you move the cursor. What am I?

   _____

9. I help artists and engineers transfer drawings from paper to the computer. What am I?

   _____

10. I am sometimes used to grade tests. What am I?

    _____

Chapter 10 ♦ Input Devices and Media

CHOOSING THE BEST EQUIPMENT FOR THE JOB

In the space provided, list the input device that best solves each problem. Give at least one reason for each choice.

1. You go to the grocery store a lot with your parents, but you really get tired of standing in line. You notice that the check-out clerk has to enter the price of each item into the cash register. You think, there must be a faster way! Then you remember, there is! What is it?

   _____
   _____
   _____
   _____
   _____
   _____

2. Your neighbors have had trouble with people breaking into their home. They have a burglar alarm that makes a noise when it is activated, but someone in the neighborhood has to call the police before they can come to the emergency. You and your neighbors discuss how nice it would be if there was a way for the police to be notified instantly when an intruder is present. Just then you remember that there is a way! What is it?

   _____
   _____
   _____
   _____
   _____
   _____

3. The store where a friend of yours works accepts credit cards. However, every time a purchase is made the credit card company must be called to make sure the card is still current and that enough credit is available to cover the purchase. The two of you discuss how much time it takes to call up the credit card company and your friend thinks out loud, "I wish there was a better way!" You just happen to have a solution. What is it?

   _____
   _____
   _____
   _____
   _____
   _____

Name _____ Class _____ Date _____

WORKING AT THE COMPUTER

Complete the following computer assignments using the software described in each assignment.

1. Use your word processor to type out the answers to the following letter scramble. Each word listed below is a type of input device. At the top of the page center the title "Input Devices." Save your document as C10A1XXX (replacing XXX with your initials). Print your document when you are finished. Type one word per line.

   yebrdako
   daldep
   chotu nrsece
   retzidigi
   rocrus
   lablacktr
   necnars
   soykictj
   semou

   > *MicroTools* Instructions:
   >
   > a. Load the *MicroTools* software and select Option 1 (Word Processing option) from the main menu.
   >
   > b. Enter the title ("Input Devices") at the top of the screen. Press <Command><C> to center the title.
   >
   > c. After you have unscrambled each of the input devices, key each device on a line of its own.
   >
   > d. Press <Command><F> to begin the File Operations command. Press <S> to save the document. Enter **C10A1XXX** (replacing XXX with your initials) as the name of the file.
   >
   > e. Press <Command><P> to begin the Print command. If you have a printer attached to your computer, press <P> to print the document to the printer. Otherwise press <S> to print it on the screen. Press <F> to print a formatted version of the document. (You will not need to do this if you are printing your document to the screen.) Press <Enter/Return> twice to tell *MicroTools* to print the entire document.
   >
   > f. Press <Command><Q> to quit the word processor and return to the main menu.
   >
   > g. Press <Esc> to exit the *MicroTools* program.

2. Use your spreadsheet program to solve the following crossword puzzle. Change the width of your columns to 3 for Columns A through O. The number of letters that each word contains is shown after each clue. If the answer is two words, do not include a blank cell between words. Save the spreadsheet as C10A2XXX (replacing XXX with your initials). Print the spreadsheet.

Down

B1: moves the cursor in all directions and is used with computerized games (8 letters)

G5: the material that information is on before being read by an input device (5 letters)

K2: used to trace maps and blueprints by architects and engineers (9 letters)

O3: ball shaped device for cursor movement (9 letters)

Across

A2: the cursor moves when this input device is rolled around on a flat surface (5 letters)

A6: draws on the screen (2 words, 8 letters)

F9: moves the cursor on the screen in horizontal and vertical directions only (6 letters)

K3: act of entering data into a computer (5 letters)

Name _____ Class _____ Date _____

MicroTools Instructions:

a. Load the *MicroTools* software and select Option 2 (Spreadsheet option) from the main menu.

b. With the cursor in Column A, press <Command><W>. Enter <3> as the new column width.

c. Repeat the instructions in Step B for Columns B though O.

d. Key the answer to each clue, beginning the word (or words) in the cell identified.

e. When all of the answers have been entered, press <Command><F> to begin the File Operations command.

Press <S> to select the Save option. Enter **C10A2XXX** (replacing XXX with your initials) as the name of the file to be saved.

f. If a printer is attached to your computer, press <Command><P> to begin the Print command. Press <P> to print the spreadsheet to the printer. Press <P> to print the spreadsheet as is.

g. Press <Command><Q> to quit the spreadsheet and return to the main menu.

h. Press <Esc> to exit the *MicroTools* program.

Name _____ Class _____ Date _____

CHAPTER 11

Output Devices and Media

COMPLETION QUESTIONS

1. _____ have the important job of delivering the final product for the computer system.
2. The _____ is one of the most frequently used output devices.
3. The most commonly used video display is the _____.
4. _____ monitors display characters in a one color pattern.
5. _____ monitors display characters in a variety of colors.
6. _____ panel displays are commonly used when a CRT cannot be used.
7. _____ flat panels are used on digital watches, calculators, electronic typewriters, and laptop and portable microcomputers.
8. _____ flat panels are used on scanners, automatic teller machines, mobile terminals in police cars, and computerized scoreboards.
9. _____ technology is used to light up the pin point lights on matrix video displays.
10. _____ are used on laptop and portable microcomputers.

81

11. _____ use a hammer-like device to strike a ribbon which leaves an inked character on the paper.
12. A _____ printer gets its name from the character "petals" on the print wheel that it uses to print one character at a time.
13. A _____ printer produces characters that appear to the reader to be made from solid lines instead of dots.
14. A _____ printer gets its name from the matrix or design of dots that is used to create one character at a time.
15. A _____ is an impact printer that uses a rotating band or belt containing characters to print a line at a time.
16. A _____ uses a rotating chain containing the characters to print a line at a time.
17. Nonimpact printers are much _____ and _____ than impact printers because there is no mechanical movement.
18. Laser printers use a _____ to form the images of the characters to be printed.
19. _____ is colored powder used by laser printers to form characters.
20. _____ printers are nonimpact printers which print a character at a time.
21. A _____ is a device that is used with a computer to generate an audio response.
22. A _____ is a device that is used with a computer to copy sounds of musical instruments and make other new and different sounds.
23. A _____ draws characters and images by using one or more pens to draw on paper.
24. A _____ plotter moves the paper under the pens to create an image.
25. The _____ on a flat-bed plotter never moves.
26. A _____ controller is a controlling device that changes computer output to some kind of action that controls a process.
27. _____ are automated devices that are designed to do specific manufacturing tasks.

Name _____ Class _____ Date _____

MATCHING EXERCISES

Match the following terms with their clues. Write the letter of each term on the appropriate line.

A. color monitor
B. daisy wheel printer
C. dot-matrix printer
D. ink-jet printer
E. band printer
F. chain printer
G. laser printer
H. plotter
I. impact
J. music synthesizer
K. nonimpact
L. real-time controller
M. voice synthesizer

1. _____ required to run some graphics software
2. _____ method that produces characters without striking the paper
3. _____ method that produces characters by actually striking the paper
4. _____ produces letter-quality type
5. _____ similar to a chain printer
6. _____ uses toner to print characters
7. _____ sprays ink onto paper
8. _____ can be used to teach music skills
9. _____ draws maps, lines, and graphics
10. _____ used on copiers, vending machines, and cars
11. _____ uses a rotating chain that contains characters
12. _____ forms characters out of rows and columns of dots
13. _____ controls mechanical parts, manufacturing equipment, and industrial robots

WHAT AM I?

In the following exercise, fill in the terms that best match the clues given.

1. I am just a soft copy when it comes to my work. What am I?

   _____

2. I strike paper but I'm really not angry. What am I?

   _____

3. I am softer and gentler and don't strike as I do my job. What am I?

   _____

4. I have a wheel that looks like a daisy but doesn't smell like one. What am I?

   _____

Chapter 11 ♦ Output Devices and Media   83

5. I am a printer that sees dots before my paper. What am I?

   _____

6. I am a kind of jet but I spray instead of fly. What am I?

   _____

7. I look and act like a copier, but I'm really a printer. What am I?

   _____

8. I am chatty but I'm not human, and I don't really have a voice. What am I?

   _____

9. I like to draw and plot my way as I work. What am I?

   _____

10. I like to be in control and tell machinery and robots what to do. What am I?

    _____

WORKING AT THE COMPUTER

Complete the following projects. You will need the *Computer Confidence* Template Disk to complete the projects that are marked with a diskette icon.

1. Load your database program. Retrieve the file called **C11A1** from the template diskette.

   The database has three fields: PRINTER, IMP/NON, and C/L/P. The **PRINTER** field lists the type of printer, such as BAND or CHAIN. The **IMP/NON** field tells if the printer is an impact printer or a nonimpact printer. The **C/L/P** field tells if the printer is a line, character, or page printer.

   Print a report of the entire database. Search the database and find out how many printers match the following categories:

Printer	No.
(1) impact printers	_____
(2) nonimpact printers	_____
(3) character printers	_____
(4) line printers	_____
(5) page printers	_____

   MicroTools Instructions:

   a. Load the *MicroTools* software and select Option 3 (Database option) from the main menu.

   b. Press <L> to load a database. Highlight **C11A1** and press <Enter/Return> to load the template file.

   c. Press <Command><R> to print a report. Press <S> to print a standard report.

Name _____ Class _____ Date _____

    d. You will be prompted to enter the order of the fields to be printed. Enter <1> in the first field (PRINTER), <2> in the second field (IMP/NON), and <3> in the third field (C/L/P).

    e. Press <Y> to tell the program that the order for printing the fields is correct.

    f. If a printer is attached to your computer, press <P> to print the report to the printer. Otherwise, press <S> to print the report to the screen.

    g. To find out how many impact printers are included in the database, press <Command><S> to begin the Search command. Press <E> to do an "Equal to" search. Enter <2> as the number for the field to search (the IMP/NON field). Enter **IMPACT** as the item to be searched for in field 2. (Make sure to enter **IMPACT** in all capital letters.) Press <D> to tell *MicroTools* that you are finished providing information about the search. Print a report of the database (follow Steps C through F if you need help printing the report). Only impact printers will be included in the report. Count the number of printers that are listed in the report and record that number in your workbook.

    h. Follow the instructions in Step G to find out how many nonimpact printers, character printers, line printers, and page printers are included in the database. In each case, you will need to tell *MicroTools* which field to search and what information should be searched for in the field.

    i. Press <Command><Q> to quit the database and return to the main menu.

    j. Press <Esc> to exit *MicroTools*.

2. Using your word processing program, write a brief report about the types of video displays that you studied in this chapter. Bold the names of the video displays whenever you refer to them. Title the report "All I've Ever Wanted to Know About Video Displays!" Write the report without copying directly from the book. Save your report as **C11A2XXX** (replacing XXX with your initials). Print the report.

    MicroTools Instructions:

    a. Load the *MicroTools* software and select Option 1 (Word Processing option) from the main menu.

    b. Key your report. Press <Command><B> before and after each word to be printed in bold. Carefully proofread your report and correct any errors you find.

c. Press <Command><F> to begin the File Operations command. Press <S> to save your report. Save the file as C11A2XXX (replacing XXX with your initials).

d. Press <Command><P> to print your report. If you have a printer attached to your computer, print the report to the printer by pressing <P> for printer. Otherwise press <S> to print to the screen. Press <F> to print a formatted version of the report. (You will not need to do this if you are printing your report to the screen). Press <Enter/Return> twice to tell *MicroTools* to print the entire report.

e. Press <Command><Q> to quit the word processor and return to the main menu.

f. Press <Esc> to exit the *MicroTools* program.

Name _____ Class _____ Date _____

CROSSWORD PUZZLE

Complete the following Crossword Puzzle. All answers to the puzzle can be found in Chapter 11 of your textbook.

Across Clues
2. monitor that uses only one color
3. a printer that uses a daisy shaped print wheel
5. a monitor that can display a wide spectrum of colors
8. a video display that does not use a CRT
9. a device that imitates the human voice
11. an output device that uses pens to draw maps on paper

Down Clues
1. print where characters appear to be made from solid lines instead of dots
4. colored powder used to form characters on a laser printer
6. a vacuum tube that produces images of characters and graphics on a monitor
7. a printer that forms characters without striking the paper
10. a printer that strikes the paper to form images

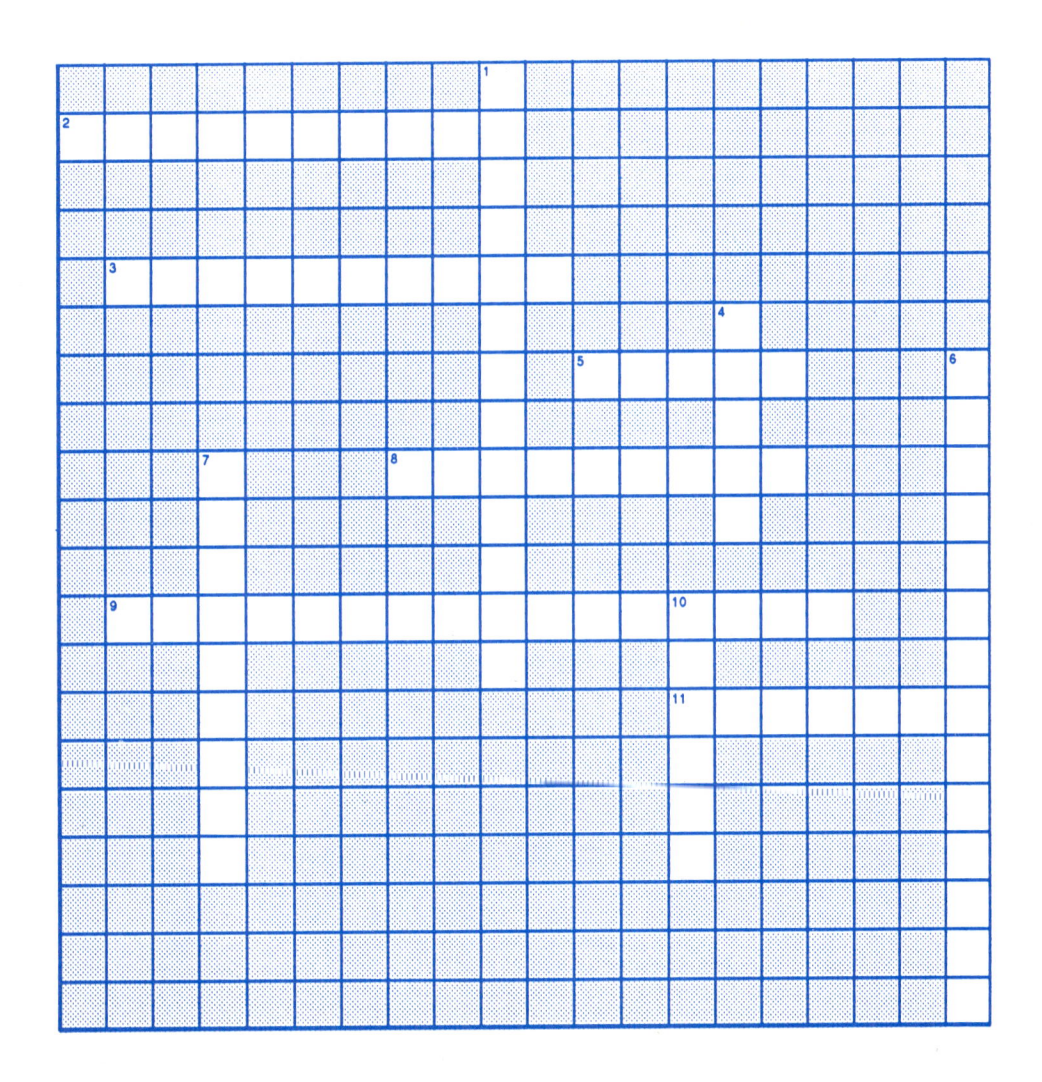

Chapter 11 ♦ Output Devices and Media

WORD SEARCH

From the scrambled letters below, find and circle the terms that match the following definitions. The terms may be read in any direction and at any angle.

1. I "firm up" the letters on a laser printer.
2. I am a diode whose first initials are LE.
3. I am a display that is flat and tubeless.
4. With me, the paper never has to move.
5. I am important; without me nobody would know the results of the computer's processing phase.
6. I am a display; when you touch me, my insides wiggle like a bowl full of gelatin.
7. When you look at me you can see how colorful I am.
8. I don't make music, I just print.
9. I'm a monitor whose name means "one color."

```
U A W E T P K R J F Z Y C F D
T T O U T P H A V W C T K L R
D E P N X N L R E N O T T A I
J A M S A L P S A G L W H T C
Y H D T B O A V E H H K N B S
T C L G I E V M V F D T B E W
L I G H T E M I T T I N G D F
I A B Y F R H D M U G G R P L
H P O U T P U T V I V E K L A
T J S P V C O L U M K V J O T
C O L O R M O N I T O R G T P
X X A Y C H A A Q S D S V I A
D Q O U I W Z H M G N M K E N
F S M O N O C H R O M E C R E
P Z B B A N D P R I N T E R L
```

CHAPTER 12

Storage Devices and Media

COMPLETION QUESTIONS

1. _____ hold data outside the memory of the computer and save it as long as desired by the user.

2. Computer designers got their ideas for computer storage from the way that information has been stored or filed in _____ in offices.

3. _____ drives store information by magnetically recording data on the surface of a spinning disk.

4. _____ means that the read/write head of a disk drive can go directly to the place on a disk where data needs to be stored or retrieved without going through all of the data that is stored on the disk.

5. _____, also known as _____, are small, bendable magnetic storage devices that are commonly used on microcomputers and minicomputers.

6. Floppy disks can be purchased in two sizes: _____ and _____.

7. A _____ is made of hard material and will not bend like a diskette.

8. If there is more than one disk in a hard disk drive they will be stacked on a _____.

89

9. The most commonly used hard disk drive on microcomputers and minicomputers uses the _____.

10. Hard disks may be either fixed or _____.

11. The _____ is a hard disk that is built onto an expansion card that is installed inside a computer.

12. A RAM drive works like a hard disk but actually uses _____ instead of disks to store data.

13. Optics is the study of _____ and _____.

14. Optical disk storage devices use _____ to burn small holes which represent the basic units of binary codes for recorded data.

15. _____ is an optical disk storage system that does not allow the user to write information on the disk.

16. Encyclopedias, ZIP-code directories, thesauruses, and dictionaries can be stored on _____ systems because they are information sources that do not require the user to update the information.

17. _____ is an interactive compact disk system that is used with television to provide audio, graphics, animation, and full-motion video for teaching students.

18. _____ is an optical disk storage system that allows the user to write information on the optical disk once and then read it as many times as needed.

19. Companies use _____ to store annual stockholder reports and financial reports for viewing in future years.

20. _____ storage technology uses magneto-optical technology to read, write, erase, and rewrite data on optical disks.

21. _____ is a long strip of flexible plastic like the tape used in a music cassette tape.

22. A _____ is a recording path along magnetic tape where the character codes are recorded.

23. With _____ the read/write head starts at the beginning of the tape and reads through all data before it finds the desired data.

24. A _____ is a plastic card that contains a built-in microchip for storing personal information.

90 Workbook ♦ *Computer Confidence: A Challenge for Today*

Name _____ Class _____ Date _____

MATCHING EXERCISES

Match the following terms with their clues. Write the letter of each term on the appropriate line.

A. read/write head
B. optical disk storage
C. CD-I
D. jukebox
E. diskette
F. sequential access
G. magnetic tape
H. random access
I. hard disk drive
J. WORM

1. ____ interacts with user by using the technology of CD-ROM and television
2. ____ used in disk drives to retrieve and store data
3. ____ also called a floppy disk
4. ____ stores and retrieves data faster than a floppy disk drive
5. ____ reads only the record wanted
6. ____ a long strip of flexible plastic
7. ____ uses a laser beam to write data
8. ____ reads data items only one after the other
9. ____ can be written on once and read many times
10. ____ changes CD-ROM disks with a robotic arm

WHAT AM I?

In the following exercise, fill in the terms that best match the clues given.

1. My name sounds like I change records, but I'm really into things that hold a lot more information. What am I?

   _____

2. I take the best of both worlds--floppy and optical--and make up my name. What am I?

   _____

3. I act tough and I work fast. I also have a large memory. What am I?

   _____

4. My name sounds like fish bait, but you can write on me one time. What am I?

   _____

5. My name sounds like I know how to study books and write stories, but I'm used by computer disk drives to retrieve and store data. What am I?

   _____

Chapter 12 ♦ Storage Devices and Media

6. I look like a credit card, but I'm much more intelligent! What am I?

   _____

7. I sound like an animal of a zodiac sign, but I'm just made out of chips. What am I?

   _____

8. I seek out what I want and go right to where it is without going through a lot of trouble. What am I?

   _____

9. That laser beam just burns me every time it wants to write something on me. What am I?

   _____

10. I attract but I'm not sticky, and I'm used to backup some computers and store for others. What am I?

    _____

WORKING AT THE COMPUTER

Complete the following projects. You will need the *Computer Confidence* Template Disk to complete the projects that are marked with a diskette icon.

1. In this activity you will use your word processing software to complete a story that has already been started for you. The story is shown below.

   Load File C12A1 from your template disk. Switch to overstrike mode and replace the blank lines with the words that are missing. When you have finished making the changes, save your document as C12A1XXX (replacing XXX with your initials). Print a copy of your document.

   > There are three types of optical disk technologies. _____ will let you read from it but will not let you write on it. _____ will let you read from it and write on it just one time. The newest technology, _____, will let you write to and read from it as many times as you want. Information is written onto all three types of these disks using a _____. All of the technologies are very fast and some of them use a _____ with a robotic arm to change disks. Users are able to use all three to look up information and someday they may replace dictionaries and other reference books.

   > *MicroTools* Instructions:
   >
   > a. Load the *MicroTools* software and select Option 1 (Word Processing option) from the main menu.

Name _____ Class _____ Date _____

    b. Press <Command><F> to begin the File Operations command. Press <L> to load a file.

    c. Highlight **C12A1** and press <Enter/Return> to load the template file.

    d. Press <Command><O> (or use the Insert key, if your computer has one) to switch to overstrike mode.

    e. Replace the blank lines with the words that are missing. When you finish, reread your story to check it for accuracy. Correct any errors that you find.

    f. Press <Command><F> to begin the File Operations command. Press <S> to save your document. Save the file as C12A1XXX (replacing XXX with your initials).

    g. Press <Command><P> to begin the Print command. If you have a printer attached to your computer, print the document to the printer by pressing <P> for printer. Otherwise, press <S>. Press <F> to print a formatted version of your document. (You will not need to do this if you are printing your document to the screen.) Press <Enter/Return> twice to tell *MicroTools* to print the entire document.

    h. Press <Command><Q> to quit the word processor and return to the main menu.

    i. Press <Esc> to exit the *MicroTools* program.

2. In this activity you will use your spreadsheet software to solve a word search puzzle. Load your spreadsheet program, and then load File C12A2. Print the spreadsheet, and then exit your spreadsheet program.

Use a pencil or pen to circle terms that appear in this chapter. You should find ten terms. If a term is made up of more than one word, it will be hidden in the puzzle without a space between words.

MicroTools Instructions:

    a. Load the *MicroTools* software and select Option 2 (Spreadsheet option) from the main menu.

    b. Press <Command><F> to begin the File Operations command. Press <L> to load a file.

    c. Highlight **C12A2** and press <Enter/Return> to load the template file.

    d. Press <Command><P> to begin the Print Operations command. Press <P> to print to printer. Press <S> to set special options. Press <N> to tell the program not to print row and column headings. Press <V> to tell the program to print values instead of formulas. Press <Enter/Return> twice to respond to the upper-left and lower-right cell to be printed entry. Press <S> to tell the program that you are using a standard printer. Press <Enter/Return> a final time and the spreadsheet will be printed.

e. After you have printed the spreadsheet, press <Command><Q> to quit the spreadsheet program and return to the main menu.

f. Press <Esc> to exit the *MicroTools* program.

g. Use a pencil or pen to circle terms that appear in this chapter. You should find ten terms. If a term is made up of more than one word, it will be hidden in the puzzle without a space between words.

```
Z A O L N V U H P G Y W D S D
V M H A R D D I S K I F G M H
B S R G R F E F F U A W E A K
R J F Z Y T T L T T O U T R H
A V W C E K T O D E P N X T L
C H N X L T E P J G D R P C M
K C J L D H K P M R O W B A A
V E H H N N S Y T C L G I R C
X V F D I B I D L V W Q P D H
O S Q X P O D I I A B Y F R A
B M U G S R T S H P D D L Z N
E V I V E K D K T J S P V C N
K E V I R D M A R R U T B N E
U Q X W K G H G X X A Y C H L
J Q S E P A T C I T E N G A M
```

Name _____ Class _____ Date _____

CROSSWORD PUZZLE

Complete the following Crossword Puzzle. All answers to the puzzle can be found in Chapter 12 of your textbook.

Across Clues
4. very similar to audio and video disks
6. compact disk, interactive
8. plastic card that contains a microchip
9. recording path on magnetic tape

Down Clues
1. small, bendable magnetic storage devices
2. compact disk, read-only memory
3. the read/write head floats above this
5. specially designed chips that work like a hard disk
7. write once, read many times

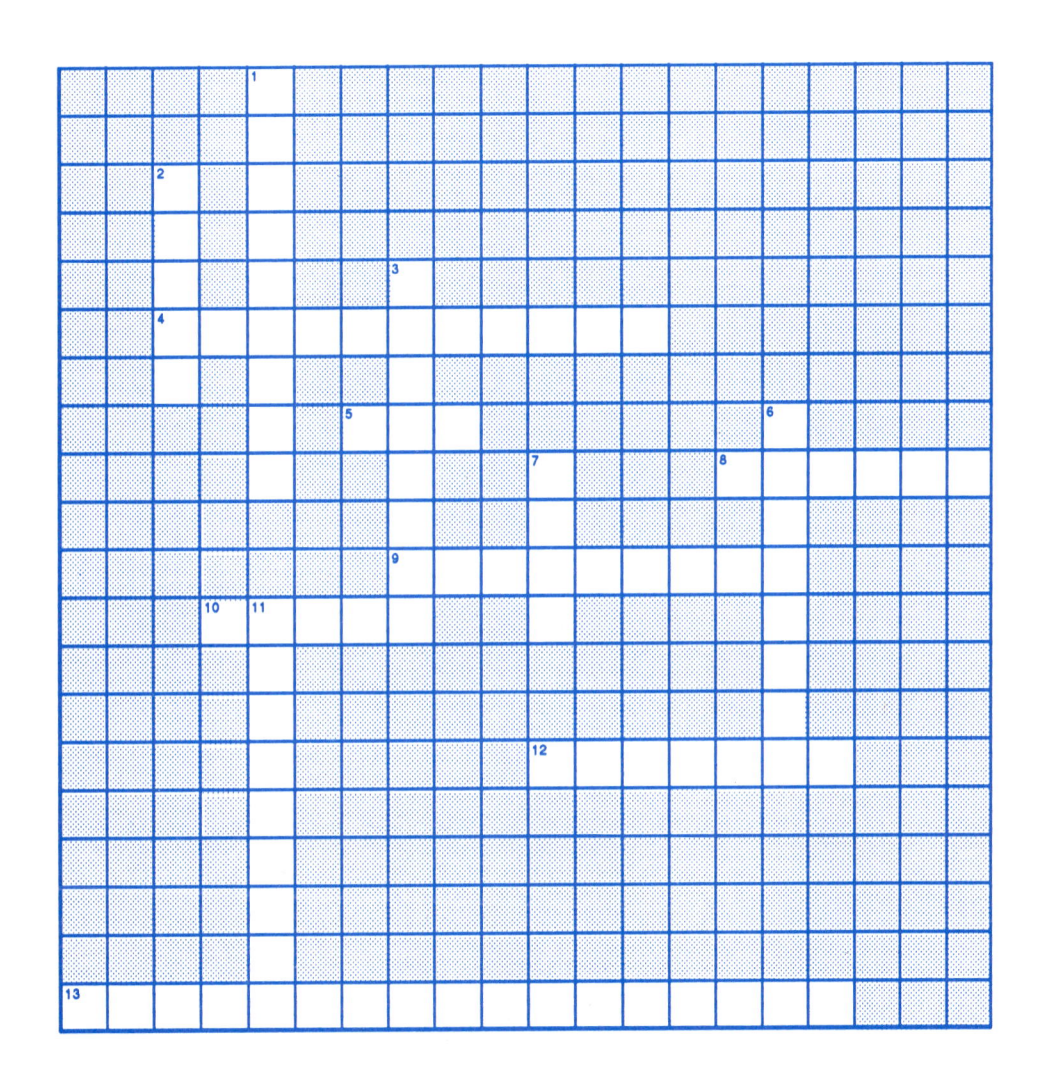

Chapter 12 ♦ Storage Devices and Media   95

Name _____ Class _____ Date _____

CHAPTER 13

Introduction to Programming

COMPLETION QUESTIONS

1. A _____ is a set of instructions that have been written in order for a computer to perform a specific task.

2. A _____ is an individual who writes computer programs.

3. The first step in the programming process is to _____ _____.

4. The second step in the programming process is to _____ _____.

5. The third step in the programming process is to _____ _____.

6. The fourth step in the programming process is to _____ _____.

7. A _____ is a chart or diagram that is used to record the different functions that a program must perform and to show the relationship of one function to another.

8. A _____ is a specific part of a program which performs a certain task.

9. A programmer can concentrate on the problem rather than special programming statements when using _____.

97

10. A flowchart uses symbols to identify certain _____ or _____.

11. The boxes or grids on a spacing chart represent lines on a _____ and/or lines on a _____.

12. A _____ is a specific set of coding instructions that is used to communicate with a computer.

13. _____ is the actual act of writing a computer program.

14. A program is coded according to the rules or _____ of the programming language that is to be used.

15. Programming mistakes are commonly called _____.

16. The act of fixing programming mistakes is called _____.

17. The programming language used in the first generation that required programmers to use the 0's and 1's of the binary code was _____.

18. The language developed during the second generation that used a concept know as automatic programming was _____.

19. A _____ is a program that translates commands that people can understand into machine language coding that a computer understands.

20. A _____ is a language that is closer to what a human understands than what a computer understands.

21. _____ was the first high-level programming language.

22. _____ was developed at Dartmouth College and was originally designed for use by students at that college.

23. _____ was developed as a teaching tool to introduce students to the computer and the logic development that is required when writing computer programs.

24. _____, commonly referred to as _____, provide automatic coding devices that allow the computer to actually write the program.

25. Fifth-generation languages use _____ which is the ability of a language to relate a series of facts and rules and propose solutions to the information given.

Name _____ Class _____ Date _____

MATCHING EXERCISES

Match the terms with their clues. Write the letter of each term on the appropriate line.

A. assembly
B. BASIC
C. C language
D. COBOL
E. 5GL
F. FORTRAN
G. 4GL
H. Logo
I. machine language
J. Pascal

1. _____ uses artificial intelligence
2. _____ developed at MIT
3. _____ has replaced BASIC in many schools
4. _____ uses 0's and 1's of binary code
5. _____ used to write system and application programs
6. _____ developed at Dartmouth College
7. _____ used in business today
8. _____ CLOUT and RAMIS are examples
9. _____ first high-level language
10. _____ second-generation language

WHAT AM I?

In the following exercise, fill in the terms that best match the clues given.

1. My name is the same as the last name of the person who invented the first mechanical adding machine, but I am a programming language. What am I?

   _____

2. I am a type of insect, but I'm also a problem to programmers. What am I?

   _____

3. I am third in the alphabet, but I was the last language to be developed during the third generation. What am I?

   _____

4. I am a programming language that is common to business and oriented to business. What am I?

   _____

5. I sound like my intelligence is not real, but I am being used as a concept for software development in the fifth generation. What am I?

   _____

Chapter 13 ♦ Introduction to Programming

6. I sound like I help people who don't speak the same language to talk with each other, but I actually help programmers "talk" with computers. What am I?

   _____

7. I am the opposite of taking the bottom-up approach, and I view things as a "big picture." What am I?

   _____

8. I sound like I am strict, but I actually provide an easy and efficient approach to programming. What am I?

   _____

9. I was developed at MIT and am used to help students learn how to design programs. I am used to draw designs, too. What am I?

   _____

10. My name sounds like I translate formulas, but I am actually the first third-generation programming language to be developed. What am I?

    _____

HIERARCHY CHART

For each of the following situations, complete a hierarchy chart.

1. Playing a video game at an arcade involves the processes of putting money into a machine and playing the game. Imagine that you have a dollar bill and need change. The video game machine that you are playing allows you to choose from a list of different games. Complete the following hierarchy chart.

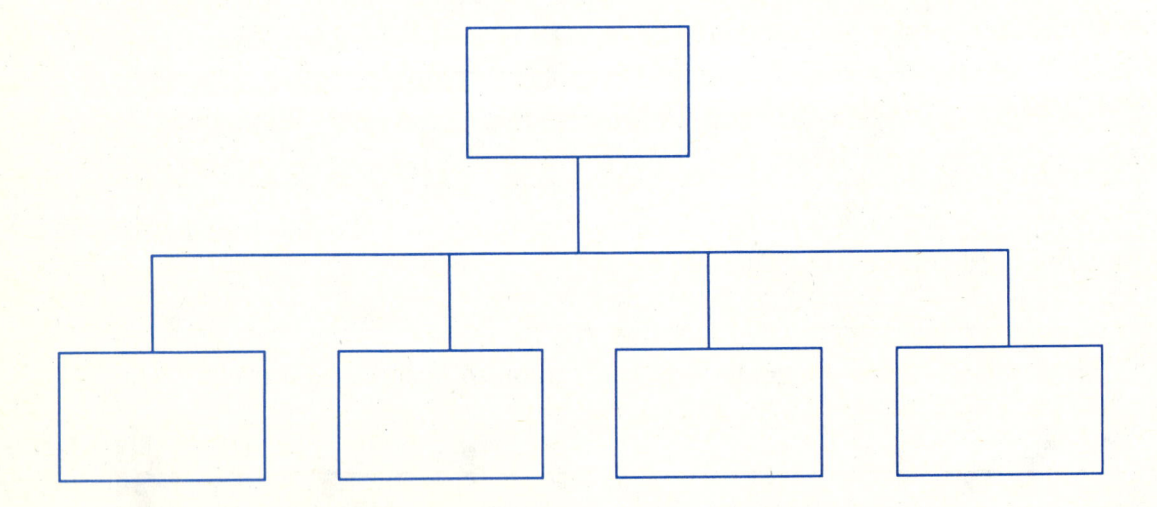

Name _____ Class _____ Date _____

2. The process of playing a cassette tape involves several steps. Can you think of what those steps would be? Complete the following hierarchy chart for the process of playing a cassette tape:

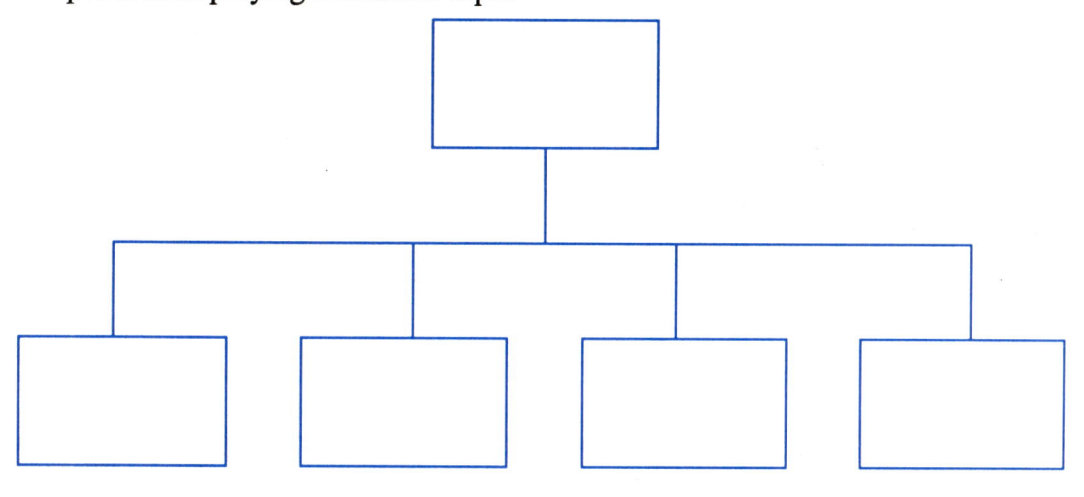

WORKING AT THE COMPUTER

Complete the following projects. You will need the *Computer Confidence* Template Disk to complete the projects that are marked with a diskette icon.

1. Your template disk contains a database file named C13A1. This file includes information about some of the programming languages discussed in Chapter 13 of your textbook. Load your database program. Then load database File C13A1.

   Each record in File C13A1 includes five fields. The field names and a description of their contents are as follows:

   LANGUAGE: This field provides the name of the language.

   GENERATION: This field indicates the generation in which the language was developed.

   APPROXDATE: This field provides the approximate date (years) in which the language was developed. In some cases, "N/A" appears instead of a date. This stands for "Not Applicable," and means that the exact date of development is not known.

   DEVELOPER: This field indicates the developer of the language. "N/A" appears if no individual, school, or company has been given credit for the development of the language.

   USE: This field indicates the typical use for the programming language.

   Print a report that includes the LANGUAGE and USE fields.

   Next, arrange the file in ascending (alphabetical) order by the LANGUAGE field (Field 1). Print a report that includes the LANGUAGE, GENERATION, and DEVELOPER fields.

Chapter 13 ♦ Introduction to Programming

Finally, search the database for all third-generation languages. Print a report of the third-generation languages that includes the LANGUAGE and GENERATION fields.

Save the database as C13A1XXX (replacing XXX with your initials).

> *MicroTools* Instructions:
>
> a. Load your *MicroTools* software. Select the Database option (Option 3).
>
> b. Press <L> to load an existing database. Highlight **C13A1** on the list of available files and press <Enter/Return> to load it.
>
> c. Press <Command><R> to print a report. Press <S> to select a standard type of report. The following prompt will appear on your screen:
>
> ---
> Enter 1 for first field to be printed, 2 for second, etc.
> ---
>
> The cursor should be in the brackets to the right of Field 1 (the LANGUAGE field). Since this is the first field to be printed, key <1> and press <Enter/Return>. The cursor will move down to Field 2. Since the next field you want to include in your report is the USE field (Field 5), do not key a number into this space. Instead, press <Enter/Return> three times to move the cursor to Field 5. Key <2> to indicate that this will be the second field included in the report and press <Enter/Return>. Your screen should look like the one shown in Figure 13.1.

```
DATABASE: C13A1              Record   1 of   8 (Max = 50)    INSERT   CAPS
                                                             Alt-H = Help
Is the order for printing the fields correct? (y or n)
..............................................................................
   1:    LANGUAGE     8 characters     [1 ]
   2:  GENERATION     1 characters     [  ]
   3:  APPROXDATE    10 characters     [  ]
   4:    DEVELOPER   25 characters     [  ]
   5:         USE    60 characters     [2 ]
```

Figure 13.1

> You must tell *MicroTools* which fields to print, as well as the order in which they should be printed.
>
> If your screen does not look like the one shown in Figure

Name _____ Class _____ Date _____

13.1, press <N> and make any necessary corrections. When your screen matches the one shown in Figure 13.1, press <Y>.

You will be asked if you want to print to the screen, file, or printer. If a printer is attached to your computer, press <P>. Otherwise, press <S> to display the report on the screen. When the report is finished printing to the screen, press the <Space Bar> to return to the database.

d. To arrange the database in ascending order, press <Command><A>. The following prompt will appear on your screen:

Arrange on which field? (1-5)

Since you want to arrange the database in ascending order on the LANGUAGE field, enter <1> as the field on which to arrange. The following prompt will appear on your screen:

Ascending or descending order? (a or d)

Press <A> to arrange the database in ascending order. Print a report of the database in its new order. Include the LANGUAGE (Field 1), GENERATION (Field 2), and DEVELOPER (Field 4) fields. If you need help printing the report, review the instructions provided in Step C.

e. Your final task is to search the database for all third-generation languages. Press <Command><S> to begin the Search command. Press <E> to perform an "Equal to" search. You will be prompted to enter the number of the field to search. Since you want to search the GENERATION field, enter <2> as the field to be searched. You will be prompted to enter the value to be searched for in the GENERATION field. Since your report is to include all third-generation languages, enter <3>. Press <D> to tell *MicroTools* that you do not want to search for any more information. Print a report that includes the LANGUAGE and GENERATION fields. (If you need help printing the report, review the instructions provided in Step C.) Only third-generation languages will appear on the report.

f. Save the database as C13A1XXX (replacing XXX with your initials).

g. Press <Command><Q> to quit the database program. Press <Esc> to exit *MicroTools*.

Chapter 13 ♦ Introduction to Programming 103

2. In this activity you will use your spreadsheet software to work with a word search puzzle that has been created as a spreadsheet program. Load your spreadsheet program, and then load File C13A2. Print the spreadsheet, and then exit your spreadsheet program.

Use a pencil or pen to circle terms that appear in this chapter. You should find 14 terms. If a term is made up of more than one word, it will be hidden in the puzzle without a space between words. The terms may be written forward or backward but will only be hidden in a horizontal (across) or vertical (up and down) direction.

MicroTools Instructions:

a. Load the MicroTools software and select Option 2 (spreadsheet) from the main menu.

b. Press <Command><F> to begin the File Operations command. Press <L> to load a file.

c. Highlight **C13A2** and press <Enter/Return> to load the template file.

d. Press <Command><P> to begin the Print Operations command.

e. Press <P> to choose printer.

f. Press <S> to set special options.

g. Press <N> to tell the program not to print row and column headings.

h. Press <V> to tell the program to print values instead of formulas.

i. Press <Enter/Return> twice to respond to the upper-left and lower-right cell to be printed entry.

j. Press <S> to tell the program that you are using a standard printer.

k. Press <Enter/Return> a final time and the spreadsheet will be printed.

l. When you have printed the spreadsheet, press <Command><Q> to quit the spreadsheet program and return to the main menu.

m. Press <Esc> to exit the *MicroTools* program.

n. Use a pencil or pen to circle terms that appear in this chapter. You should find 14 terms. If a term is made up of more than one word, it will be hidden in the puzzle without a space between words. The terms may be written forward or backward but will only be hidden in a horizontal (across) or vertical (up and down) direction.

Name _____ Class _____ Date _____

CHAPTER 14

Logo

COMPLETION QUESTIONS

1. In order to give instructions to the turtle, Logo uses a language known as _____.

2. A _____, also referred to as a command, is an instruction that tells the turtle what to do.

3. Procedures that the turtle already knows are called _____ _____ or just _____.

4. _____ are procedures that are created by the user by combining several primitives.

5. _____ is a procedure that makes the turtle appear on the screen.

6. _____ is a procedure that commands the Logo program to make the turtle disappear.

7. _____ is a procedure that commands the Logo program to clear the screen of all turtle tracks and return the turtle to the center of the screen.

8. _____ is a procedure that commands the Logo program to clear the screen of all turtle tracks and leave the turtle in the same position it was in before the CLEAN command was entered.

9. _____ is a procedure that commands the Logo program to clear the text area of the screen.

10. The _____ primitive causes the turtle to turn right a specified number of degrees.

11. The _____ primitive causes the turtle to turn left a specified number of degrees.

12. The _____ primitive causes the turtle to move forward a specified number of steps.

13. A _____ is a unit of measurement used when measuring angles or the distance between two lines connected at a point.

14. A circle has _____ degrees.

15. The _____ command tells Logo to repeat primitives or procedures a certain number of times.

16. The _____ command causes the turtle to "lift" its pen so that it will not draw lines as it moves.

17. The _____ command causes the turtle to "put" its pen down so that it will draw lines as it moves.

18. The _____ command allows the user to edit a user-defined procedure.

19. The _____ command is used to save procedures created during a work session.

20. The _____ command is used to load procedures into memory from disk.

21. The _____ command is used to erase a procedure from memory.

22. The _____ primitive backs the turtle up without the turtle point changing its directions.

23. The _____ command transforms the turtle from a pen to an eraser.

24. The _____ command causes the turtle to erase any line that has previously been drawn and draw where there was no line before.

FIGURING THE ANGLE

In the exercises on the following pages, the turtle is shown in five positions. In each problem, draw the turtle to show the position it would be in after it moved according to the primitive given.

Name ______________________ Class __________ Date ____________

Current Position | **Primitive** | **New Position**

Example

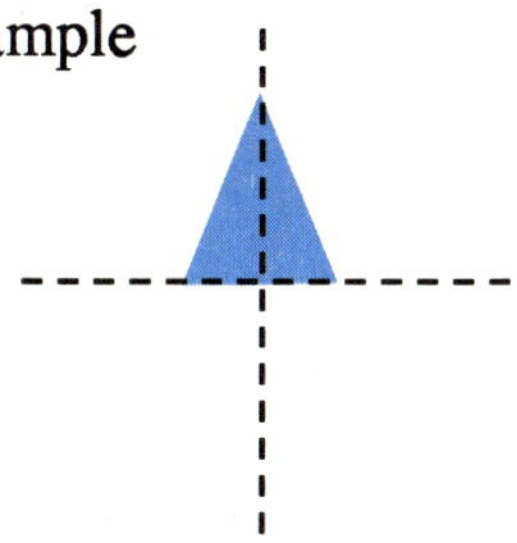

LT 180

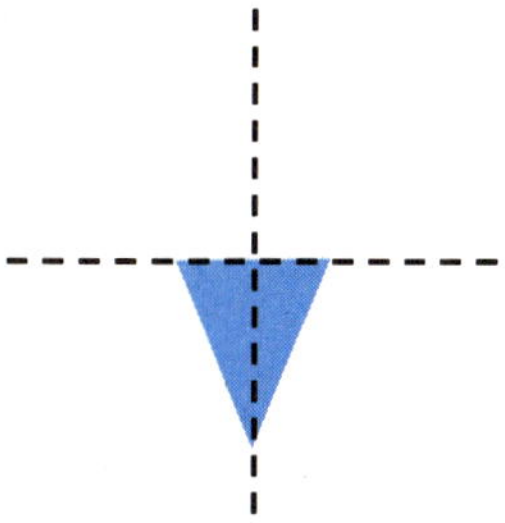

1.

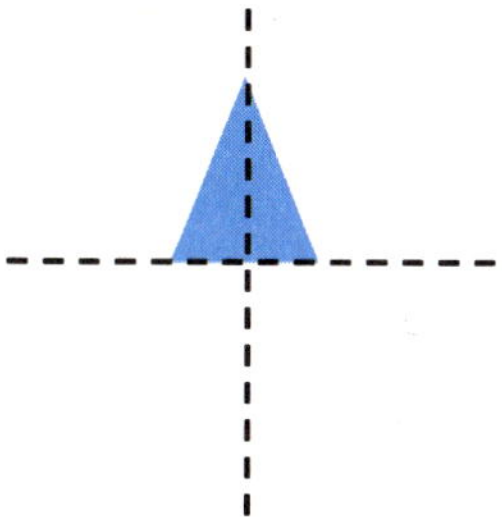

RT 90

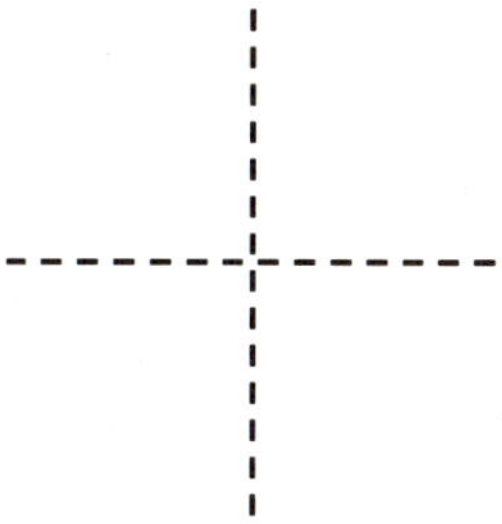

2.

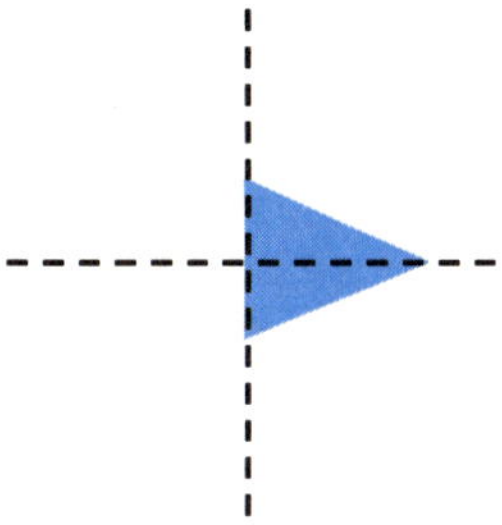

LT 90

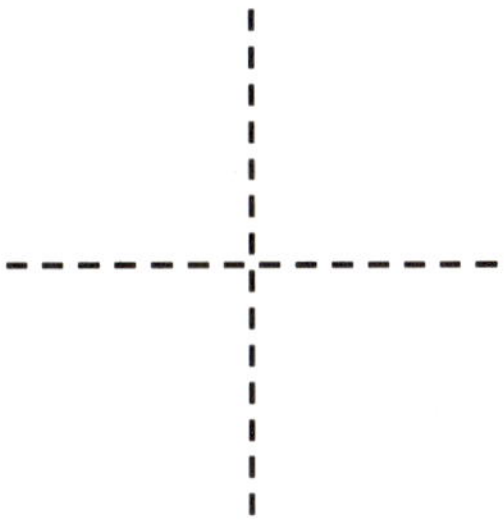

3.

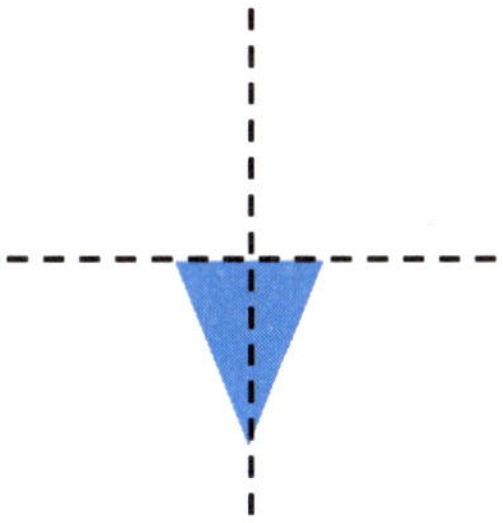

RT 90

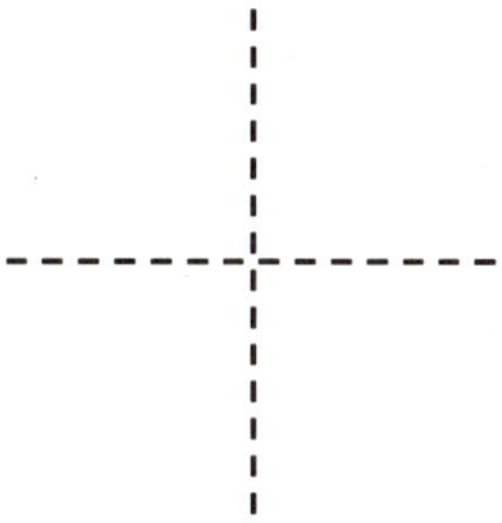

4.

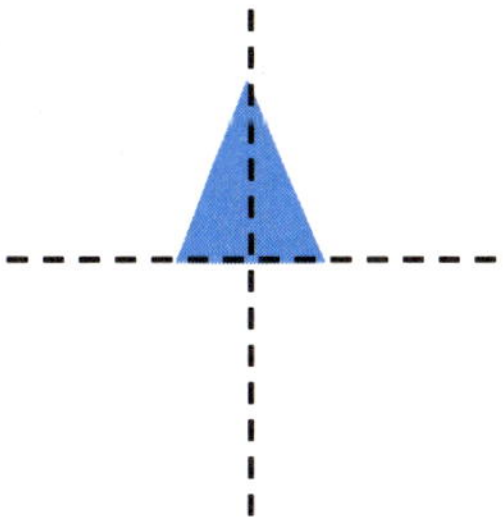

RT 180

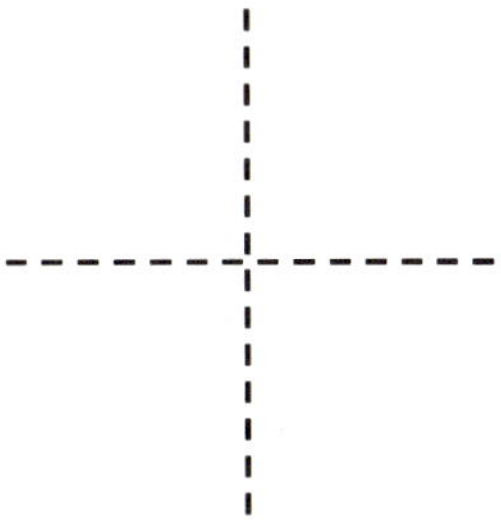

(Exercise continued)

Current Position	Primitive	New Position

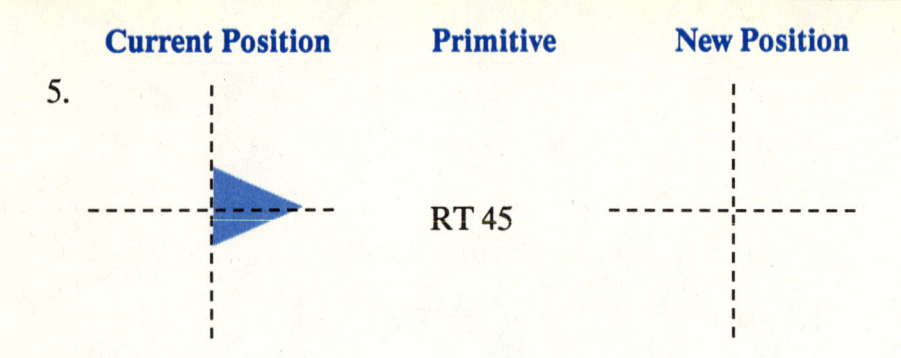

5.   RT 45

YOU BE THE TURTLE

In the following exercises, imagine that you are the turtle. Using a pencil, draw the turtle tracks that Logo would draw. The work space provided has been divided into grids. Each section of the grid represents one step of the turtle. The circle indicates the starting point of the turtle. Assume the turtle is pointing straight up as it is on the Logo screen when you first begin. When you have finished drawing, draw an arrow beside the design to indicate which direction the turtle is pointing when you finish drawing the design. (NOTE: If you key these examples in using your Logo program, the shapes will be different since the turtle tracks on the screen are different than the grids on the worksheets provided.)

1. FD 5
    RT 90
    FD 5
    RT 90
    FD 5
    RT 90
    FD 5

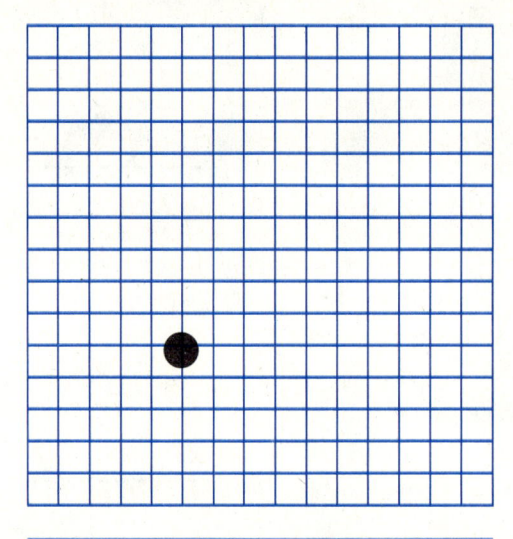

2. FD 2
    RT 90
    FD 2
    LT 90
    FD 2
    RT 90
    FD 2
    LT 90
    FD 2
    RT 90

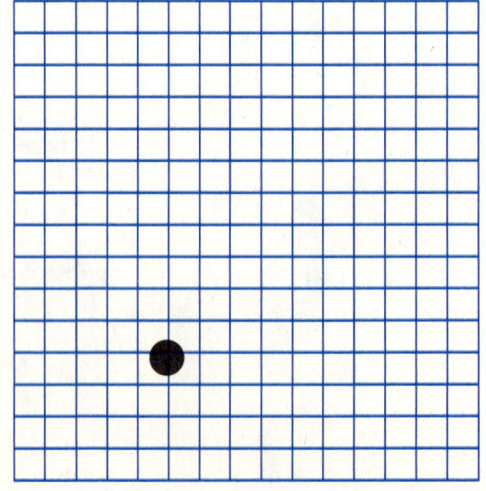

110　　　　　　　　　　Workbook ♦ *Computer Confidence: A Challenge for Today*

Name _____ Class _____ Date _____

3. FD 2
   LT 90
   FD 4
   RT 90
   FD 2
   RT 90
   FD 4
   LT 90
   FD 2
   RT 90
   FD 3
   RT 90
   FD 2
   LT 90
   FD 4
   RT 90
   FD 2
   RT 90
   FD 4
   LT 90
   FD 2
   RT 90
   FD 3

4. FD 2
   RT 90
   FD 2
   RT 90
   FD 2
   RT 90
   FD 2
   PU
   FD 4
   PD
   FD 3
   RT 90
   FD 2
   RT 90
   FD 3
   RT 90
   FD 2
   PU
   FD 2
   PD
   LT 90
   FD 4
   RT 90
   FD 3
   RT 90
   FD 4
   RT 90
   FD 3

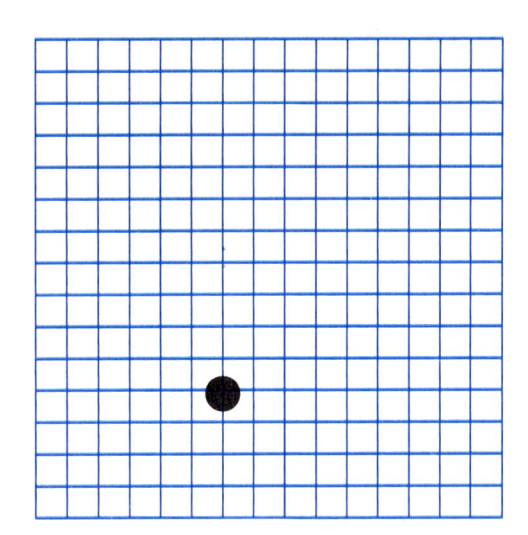

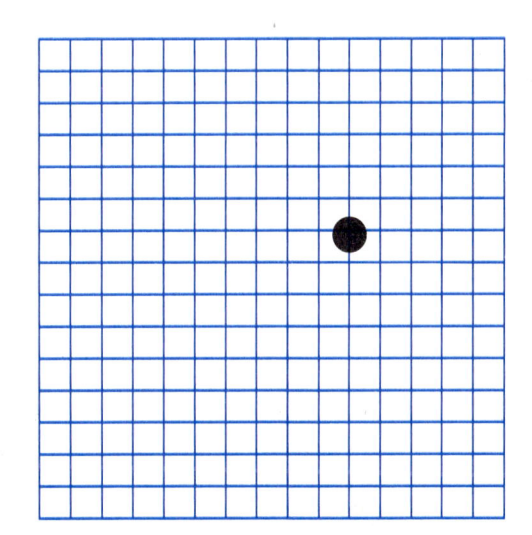

Chapter 14 ♦ Logo

5. REPEAT 4 [FD 5 RT 90]

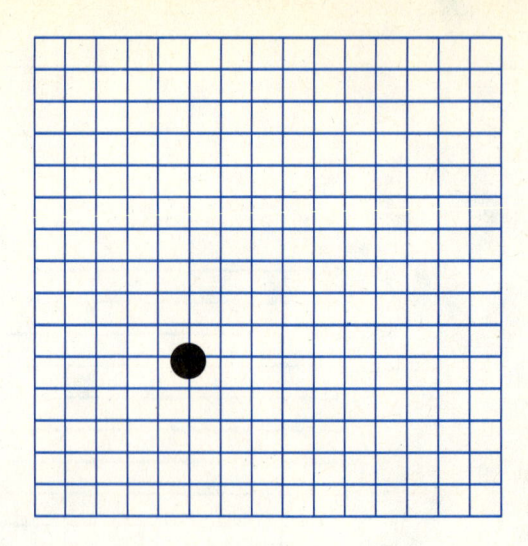

6. FD 4
   RT 90
   FD 4
   BK 2
   LT 90
   FD 2
   RT 90
   FD 2
   RT 90
   FD 2
   LT 90
   FD 2
   RT 90
   FD 4
   RT 90
   FD 4
   BK 2
   RT 90
   FD 1
   LT 90
   FD 2
   LT 90
   FD 1
   RT 90
   FD 2

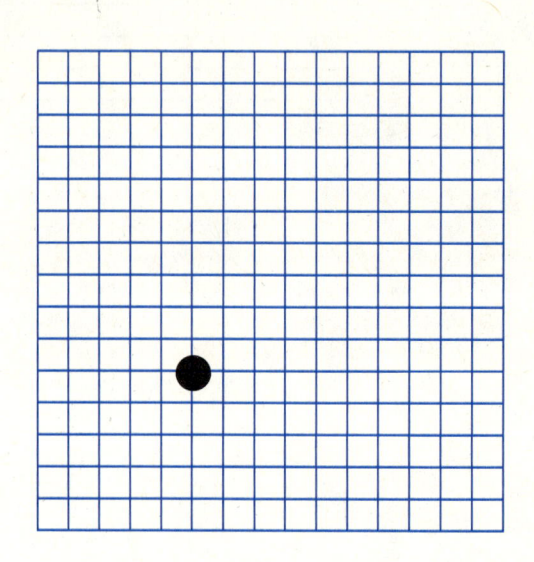

WORKING AT THE COMPUTER

The following computer activities are designed to be used with Logo. Study each design carefully and write a procedure to produce the design shown in each activity. Key in your procedure using your Logo program. Try to match the examples as closely as possible.

1. The design shown on the top of the next page is made by drawing four circles. Write a procedure to draw the four circles by beginning with the largest circle first and then the next smallest. Remember that circles have 360°. Each circle is one-half the size of the one previously drawn.

Name _____ Class _____ Date _____

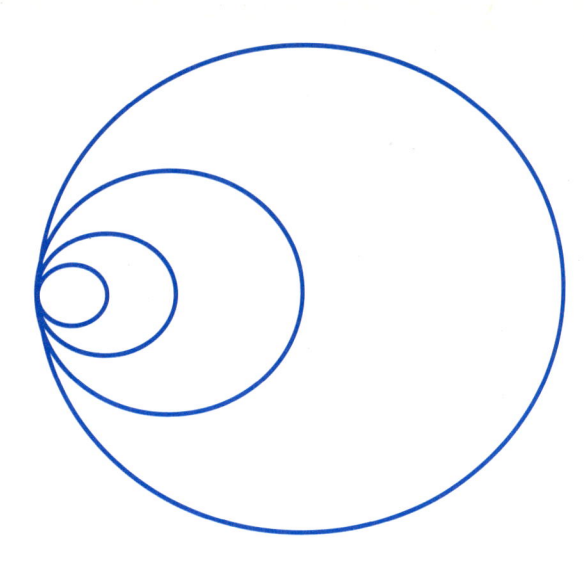

2. The design shown below is made by drawing seven squares. Write a procedure to draw the seven squares by beginning with the largest square first and then the next smallest. Each square in this design is five steps smaller than the previous square.

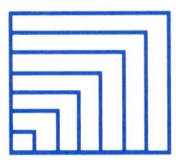

3. The design shown below is made by drawing one side of a triangle, turning $120°$, then drawing another side of the triangle five steps larger, turning $120°$, etc. Beginning at the center, the first line is five steps long, the second line is ten steps long, etc. Write a procedure to draw the 18 lines that make up this design.

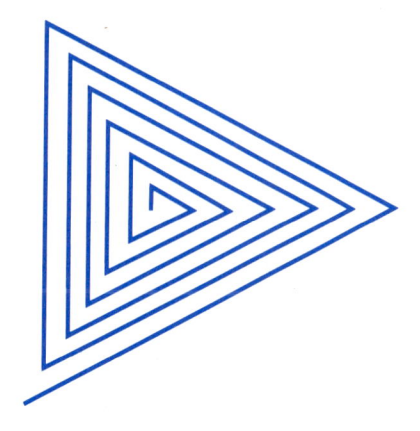

4. The design shown at the top of the next page is made by drawing five squares, one inside the other. Start with the smallest square and make each new square 15 steps larger than the previous one. Be sure to PENUP after each square, change the position of the turtle, then PENDOWN before you

Chapter 14 ♦ Logo

draw the next square. A left turn of 135° after each square with a FD 10 primitive will position the turtle to draw the next square. Be sure, though, that you turn the turtle back to the right 135° before drawing the next square.

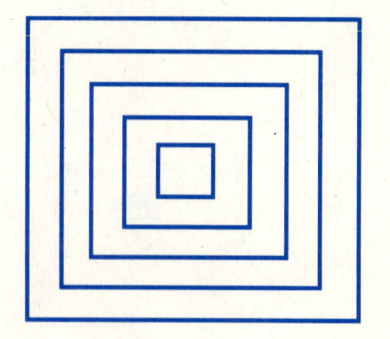

Name _____ Class _____ Date _____

CHAPTER 15

Programming in BASIC

COMPLETION QUESTIONS

1. The step-by-step instructions that a computer needs in order to function are commonly called a _____.
2. Programs are written by _____.
3. BASIC stands for _____ _____.
4. BASIC was developed at Dartmouth College in the mid-1960s by _____ and _____.
5. The BASIC programming language is very similar to the English language and uses English language words called _____.
6. In BASIC, each programming instruction that is keyed in is called a _____.
7. A keyword that tells the computer to take an immediate action is called a _____.
8. The NEW command _____.
9. The _____ command causes the BASIC interpreter to run or execute the program.
10. The LIST command provides a numerically ordered listing on the _____ of each statement that has been keyed.
11. The LLIST command provides a numerically ordered listing on the _____ of each statement that has been keyed.

115

12. The _____ command causes one or more lines from a BASIC program to be deleted.
13. The _____ command will cause the program in memory to be saved or stored on disk.
14. The _____ command reads the program that is on disk and loads it into memory.
15. The _____ keyword tells the computer to print output on the screen.
16. A _____ is information that needs to be printed exactly as it is keyed.
17. A _____ is a number that can be treated mathematically.
18. Operators are special symbols used to perform _____ _____.
19. An expression is formed by combining _____ with _____.
20. The _____ keyword tells the computer to print output on the printer.
21. The _____ keyword is used to allow remarks to be placed in the program.
22. The _____ keyword is used to mark the end of a BASIC program.
23. _____ are names that the program provides for locations in memory where data will be stored.
24. Variable names used to store characters should end with a _____ sign (called a _____).
25. The keyword _____ allows information to be keyed into variables from the keyboard.

BASICALLY SPEAKING

Provide an answer to the following expressions based on how BASIC performs math calculations.

1. 10 PRINT (35 + 15) / 2 * 3   1. _____
2. 10 PRINT 8 + 6 / 2 * 3   2. _____
3. 10 PRINT 12 + 3 + 5 - 6 * 3   3. _____
4. 10 PRINT 5*((2+3)*2)+7   4. _____
5. 10 PRINT (8 + 34 + 2)/2*2   5. _____

Name _____ Class _____ Date _____

FROM PSEUDOCODE TO BASIC

In the exercise below, there are four program designs for four different problems that have been written in pseudocode. In the space provided, write the BASIC code for each problem. Start each problem with Line 10. You may make up data that is not provided. Provide both the BASIC code for the problem and the expected output of the problem. You will need to use several BASIC statements in each problem. Once you have completed the exercise in the workbook, key in your programs to see if they produce the desired output.

Problem 1
a. Store the value 25 in variable A and the value 50 in variable B.
b. Add the numbers together and store them in variable C.
c. Describe the answer and print the contents of variable C on the screen.

BASIC Code:
_____
_____
_____
_____
_____
_____
_____

Output:
_____
_____

Problem 2
a. Get name of user from keyboard.
b. Get age of user from keyboard.
c. Multiply age by 365 to provide the approximate number of days the user has lived and store that number in a variable.
d. Print the answer on the screen with a statement describing the output.

BASIC Code:
_____
_____
_____
_____
_____
_____
_____

Output:
_____
_____
_____

Chapter 15 ♦ Programming in BASIC

Problem 3

a. Get name of user from keyboard.
b. Get favorite color of user from keyboard.
c. Get favorite animal of user from keyboard.
d. Get favorite TV show of user from keyboard.
e. Get name of city of user from keyboard.
f. Print the information about the user in a creative way on the screen.

BASIC Code:

Output:

Name _____ Class _____ Date _____

Problem 4
a. Ask the user to input two numbers and store them in variables. Tell the user what the program is going to do before they begin inputting data.
b. Multiply the numbers and store the answer in a variable.
c. Divide the numbers and store the answer in a variable.
d. Print the product of the two numbers with an explanation.
e. Print the quotient of the two numbers with an explanation.

BASIC Code:
_____
_____
_____
_____
_____
_____
_____
_____
_____
_____
_____
_____

Output:
_____
_____
_____
_____
_____
_____
_____
_____

YOU BE THE COMPUTER

Pretend like you are a computer. Instead of keying the following programs into your computer, use the grids provided to supply the output that you think the following BASIC program will supply.

1.  ```
    10 REM *** THIS IS A PROGRAM THAT ADDS TWO NUMBERS ***
    20 LET A = 5
    30 LET B = 10
    40 LET C = A + B
    50 PRINT "THE SUM IS ";C
    60 END
    ```

2.  ```
    10 PRINT "H E L L O"
    20 PRINT "I"
    30 PRINT "A M"
    40 PRINT "A"
    50 PRINT "C O M P U T E R"
    60 END
    ```

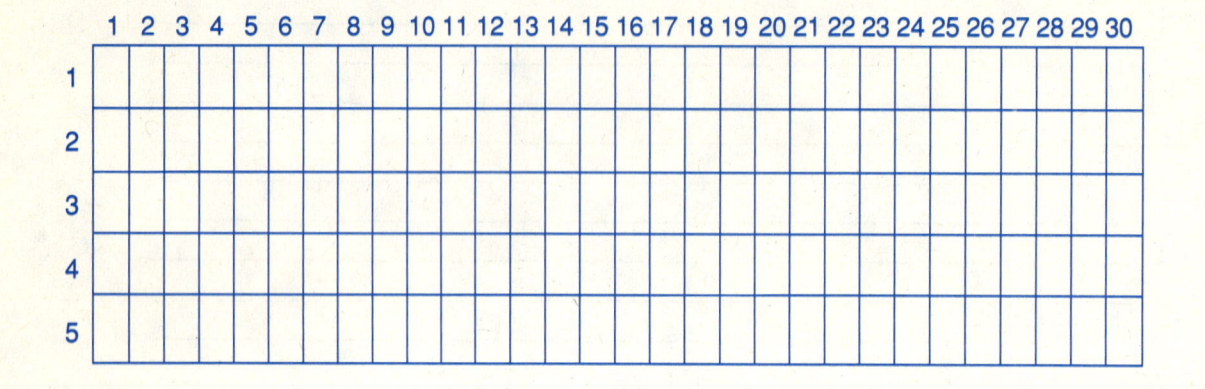

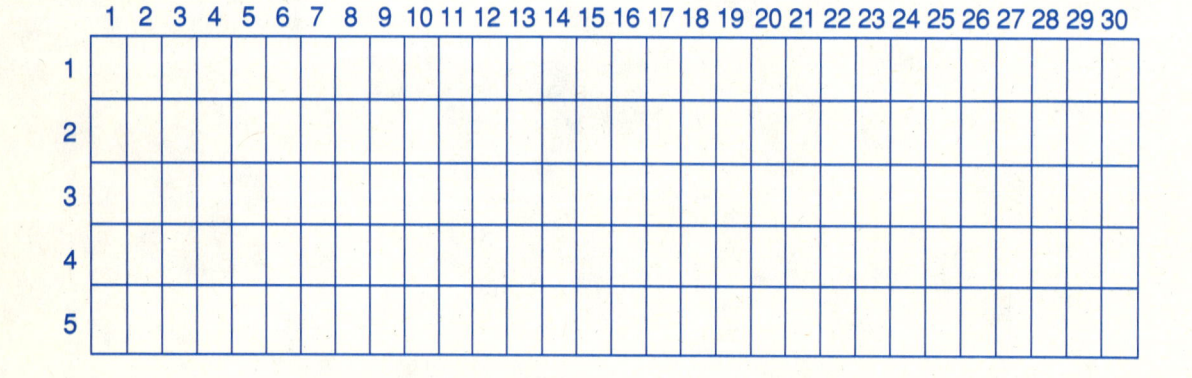

3.
```
10 REM *** THIS PROGRAM DOES MATH ***
20 PRINT "5 + 4 / 2 = "
30 PRINT 5 + 4 / 2
40 PRINT "8 + 12 / 2 * 5 = "
50 PRINT 8 + 12 / 2 * 5
60 REM *** END OF PROGRAM ***
70 END
```

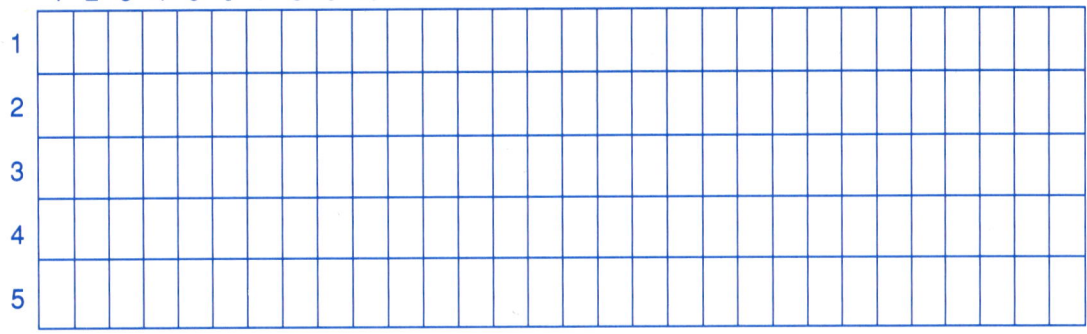

4.
```
10 PRINT "NAME", "JOHN", "SUE"
20 PRINT "AGES", "12", "8"
30 PRINT "THEY ARE MY FRIENDS"
40 END
```

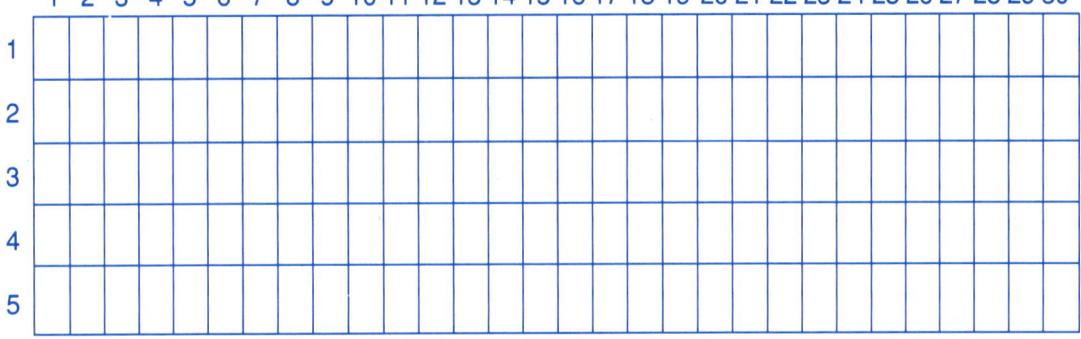

5.
```
10 LET A = 5
20 LET B = 6
30 LET C = 7
40 LET D = A + B
50 PRINT C
```

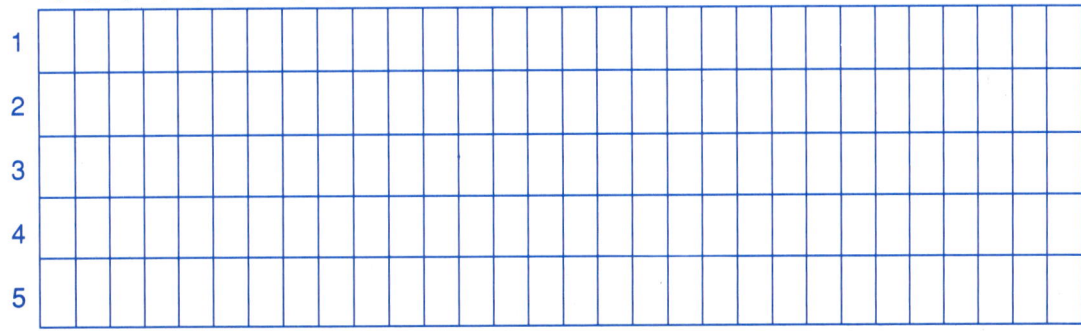

Chapter 15 ♦ Programming in BASIC

WORKING AT THE COMPUTER

Write the following BASIC programs and key them into your computer. Save each program and print a copy of each program. Start each program with Line 10 and provide REM statements to identify the program number and your name.

1. Write a BASIC program that produces a listing of salespeople, their total sales, and their total commissions. Use commas in your print statements to arrange the output in zones. The output should look like the following:

   Sales Report

Name	Sales	Commissions
Craig Jordon	450	22.50
Lu Huang	795	53.95
Jane Gray	800	40.00
Beth Wallace	300	12.50

2. Using the program written in Problem 1, add a total line to the output. You will need to add statements to calculate the total of the sales and the total of the commissions.

Name _____ Class _____ Date _____

3. Write a program that will print the sum of the numbers 25 and 50.

4. Write a program that will add, subtract, multiply and divide any two numbers keyed in from the keyboard. Be sure to explain your answers.

5. On the next page, write a program to allow a salesperson to input the name of a customer and the amount of an item purchased. The program should figure the amount of tax on the item purchased and compute the total owed. The program should print a receipt for the customer showing his or her name, amount of purchase, amount of tax, and total amount to be collected. Assume that a 7% sales tax will be charged. (Hint: Use as .07 in the formula.) The output should look similar to the following:

    RECEIPT FOR JOHN JONES

    AMOUNT PURCHASED   300.00
          SALES TAX   21.00
          TOTAL DUE   321.00

    THANK YOU FOR SHOPPING WITH US!

Chapter 15 ♦ Programming in BASIC

Name _____ Class _____ Date _____

CHAPTER 16

Computers, Careers, and You

COMPLETION QUESTIONS

1. There is no part of society that has not been touched by the _____.

2. Before a computer ever reaches the public and is available for sale, the product goes through an enormous amount of _____ _____.

3. _____ work for computer manufacturers and are responsible for many of the exciting inventions that have occurred in the computer industry.

4. _____ programs are used to allow the engineer to do design work on the computer.

5. Once the research and development stages are completed, the computer design enters the _____ stage.

6. Every computer manufacturer has _____ who talk with possible customers about the features of the computer.

7. _____ are trained to replace parts and to check for problems in the operation of the computer.

8. System programmers write instructions that tell the computer _____ _____.

9. Application programmers write instructions to _____ _____.

125

10. A _____ prepares written manuals to explain how to use a particular type of computer and how to run software programs.

11. _____ travel to companies that buy their products and train workers to use new computer equipment.

12. Payroll clerks use the computer to _____ _____.

13. Doctors use computers to _____ _____.

14. As _____ and _____ systems become more widely available, workers will be able to talk to computers.

15. The size of computers, floppy disks, and peripherals will continue to get _____ while the memory capacities of computers and the storage capacities of disks will continue to get _____.

MATCHING EXERCISES

Match the following terms with their clues. Write the letter of each term on the appropriate line.

A. application programmer
B. computer engineer
C. computer scientist
D. customer service representative
E. computer service technician
F. technical writer

1. _____ person who repairs computers
2. _____ person who tests and tries new designs
3. _____ person who teaches others how to use computers
4. _____ person who writes instructions in manuals
5. _____ person who plans and designs computer parts
6. _____ person who writes programs that solve problems

IDENTIFYING EDUCATION AND JOB SKILLS

For each job title listed below, fill in the education required and at least one job skill needed.

1. Computer Scientist: _____
   _____
   _____
   _____
   _____
   _____

Name _____ Class _____ Date _____

2. Computer Engineer: _____
   _____
   _____
   _____
   _____
   _____

3. Manufacturing Worker: _____
   _____
   _____
   _____
   _____
   _____

4. Computer Salesperson: _____
   _____
   _____
   _____
   _____
   _____

5. Customer Service Representative: _____
   _____
   _____
   _____
   _____
   _____

IDENTIFYING CAREERS

Fill in each blank with the career that best matches each description given.

1. If you like working with your hands and repairing things, what computer career would best fit your interests? _____
   _____

2. If you understand what computers can do and what they cannot do and have the patience to discover what other people want, what computer career would best fit your interests? _____
   _____

Chapter 16 ♦ Computers, Careers, and You

3. If you like to teach others and work with computers, what computer career would best fit your interests? _____

4. If you have always enjoyed making and designing things, what computer career would best fit your interests? _____

5. If you are very creative and like testing and trying out ideas and inventing new things, which computer career would best fit your interests? _____

6. If you like working with details and like writing step-by-step instructions, which computer career would best fit your interests? _____

WORKING AT THE COMPUTER

Complete the following projects. You will need the *Computer Confidence* Template Disk to complete the projects that are marked with a diskette icon.

1. In this activity you will use your word processing software to complete a story that has already been started for you. The story is shown in Figure 16.1. Load File C16A1 from your template diskette. Switch to the overstrike mode and replace the blank lines with words that are missing. When you are finished making changes, save your document as C16A1XXX (replacing XXX with your initials). Print a copy of your document.

> *MicroTools* Instructions:
>
> a. Load the *MicroTools* software and select Option 1 (Word Processing option) from the main menu.
>
> b. Press <Command><F> to begin the File Operations command. Press <L> to load a file.
>
> c. Highlight **C16A1** and press <Enter/Return> to load the template file.
>
> d. Press <Command><O> (or use the Insert key, if your computer has one) to switch to overstrike mode.
>
> e. Replace the blank lines with the career titles that are missing. When you finish, reread your story to check it for accuracy. Correct any errors that you find.
>
> f. Press <Command><F> to begin the File Operations command. Press <S> to save your document. Save the file as C16A1XXX (replacing XXX with your initials).
>
> g. Press <Command><P> to begin the Print command. If you have a printer attached to your computer, print the

Name _____ Class _____ Date _____

LAND OF PC

Once upon a time there was a place known as the Land of PC. The Land of PC was a very busy place and everyone who worked there had computer careers. Mr. Database was a problem solver. He was responsible for writing programs to solve problems. He held the job of _____ _____. Miss Teachit, the _____ _____, worked with other people in her company and trained them on how to use computers. She also trained people who bought computers from her company. Miss Techi was a stickler for detail. She worked and worked at getting the step-by-step instructions right for her manuals. Her career title was _____ _____. Mr. Instruct thought his job was the most important one of all. He wrote programs that would tell the computer how to operate. His career title was _____ _____. Mr. Fixit loved to work on computers. He was responsible for repairing all the computers when they broke. His career title was _____ _____. Miss Invent spent all her time in the research and development lab trying out new ideas and testing new techniques. She loved her work. Her job title was _____ _____. Mr. Designit worked very closely with Miss Invent. He would plan and design all the parts needed to build the computers that Miss Invent dreamed up. Mr. Designit worked as a _____ _____ in the Land of PC. Never before has a place had as much impact on the world of business as the Land of PC.

Figure 16.1
File C16A1

document to the printer by pressing <P> for printer. Otherwise press <S> to print to the screen. Press <F> to print a formatted version of your document. (You will not need to do this if you are printing your document to the screen.) Press <Enter/Return> twice to tell *MicroTools* to print the entire document.

h. Press <Command><Q> to quit the word processor and return to the main menu.

i. Press <Esc> to exit the *MicroTools* program.

2. In this activity you will work with a database file that has already been created for you. This file, named C16A2, contains five fields. The field names and their contents are as follows:

CAREER--This field identifies the career about which information is contained in the record.

TECH SKILL--This field indicates whether or not technical skills are required for the career identified in Field 1. A "Yes" in this field means that technical skills are required for the career.

PEOPLE SKL--This field indicates whether or not "people" skills are required for the career identified in Field 1. A "Yes" in this field means that people skills are required for the career. A "No," however, does not mean that people skills are not required. It simply means that people skills are not as important as technical skills for success in the career.

EDUCATION--This field identifies the educational requirements for the career listed in Field 1.

JOB DESCRP--This field provides a brief description of the career identified in Field 1.

Load your database software and retrieve File C16A2. Print a report of all of the records in the original file. Include all five fields of each record in your report. Sort the file alphabetically by the CAREER field. Print a report of the database in the new order. Again, include every field of each record in the report.

Next, search the file for all careers that require technical skills but do not require people skills and print a report of these careers. Finally, search the file for all careers which require people skills and print a report containing those careers.

MicroTools Instructions:

a. Load your *MicroTools* program disk and select the Database option (Option 3).

b. Press <L> to load a database. Highlight **C16A2** and press <Enter/Return>.

c. Press <Command><R> to begin the Report command. Press <N> to select the New option. You will be prompted to enter 1 for the first field to be printed, 2 for the second field to be printed, and so on. Enter <1> in the CAREER field, 2 in the TECH SKILL field, and so on, until the print order for all five fields has been specified. You will be asked to indicate if the order for printing the fields is correct. When the order for printing the fields is correct, press <Y>. For each of the prompts indicated, answer with the response provided in the "< >" brackets:

Are you printing mailing labels? <*N*>
Print field names? <*Y*>
Enter number of lines to skip between records: <*1*>
Enter tab position for CAREER: <*1*>
Enter tab position for TECH SKILL: <*40*>
Enter tab position for PEOPLE SKL: <*55*>
Enter tab position for EDUCATION: <*1*>
Enter tab position for JOB DESCRP: <*1*>
Enter number of calculated fields: <*0*>
Save this report format? <*Y*>
Enter filename for report format: <*C16A2XXX*> (replace XXX with your initials)

Name _____ Class _____ Date _____

You will be asked if the report should be printed to the screen, file, or printer. If a printer is attached to your computer, press <P> to print the report to the printer. Otherwise press <S> to print the report to the screen.

d. Arrange (sort) the file by the Career field by pressing <Command><A>. Choose <1> for the field to arrange and <A> for ascending order. Press <Command><R> to begin the Report command. Press <E> to select the Existing report option. Press <L> to load an existing report format. Highlight C16A2XXX and press <Enter/Return>. If a printer is attached to your computer press <P> to print the report to the printer. Otherwise press <S> to print the report to the screen.

e. Search the file for all careers that require technical skills but do not require people skills by pressing <Command><S>. Choose <E> for equal to and enter <2> for the field number to be searched. Enter **YES** as the value to be searched for, and then press <A> for and. Press <E> for equal to and enter <3> for the field number to be searched. Enter **NO** as the value to be searched for. Print the report following the instructions in Step D.

f. Search the file for all careers that require people skills by pressing <Command><S>. Press <E> for equal to and enter <3> to search Field 3. Enter **YES** as the value to be searched for, and then press <D> for done. Print the report following the instructions in Step D.

g. Press <Command><Q> to quit the database and return to the main menu. Do not save the database file.

h. Press <Esc> to exit *MicroTools*.

Chapter 16 ♦ Computers, Careers, and You

APPENDIX A

Start-up Procedures

APPLE START-UP PROCEDURES

FOR *MICROTOOLS: INTEGRATED SOFTWARE FOR WORD PROCESSING, SPREADSHEET, AND DATABASE*

The start-up procedures for the Apple IIe, Apple IIc, and Apple IIGS microcomputers are as follows:

Step 1 Turn on the monitor.

Step 2 Open the door to Disk Drive 1 and carefully insert your *MicroTools* program diskette #1.

Step 3 Close the door to the disk drive.

Step 4 If the computer is off, turn on all power switches. If the computer is already on, hold down <Control>, the Open Apple key, and <Reset> at the same time. This will boot the system, and the computer will be ready for use.

Step 5 After a short pause, four screens displaying copyright information will appear. Press <Return> four times to move through these displays. The Main Menu will appear.

Step 6   Select Change System Features.

Step 7   If the drive specification currently set in Menu Item 1 of the Change System Features menu refers to the volume that you wish to save your data files to, go to Step 8. If it is not, enter a **1**. You will be prompted to enter a path name that matches the name on the data/template diskette or press <Return>. (Ask your instructor for the path name you are to use.)

Note: Before you can save data files to your data diskette, the diskette must be formatted. (For information on formatting a diskette, ask your teacher for assistance.)

Step 8   If the printer type currently set in Menu Item 2 of the Change System Features menu is the type of printer you will be using, press <Esc>. If it is not, enter a **2**. Select the desired printer type by keying the appropriate menu choice. Then return to the main menu by pressing <Esc>.

Note: If your printer is not listed, you will need to customize the software for your printer by keying the codes required for bold and underline print modes via Menu Item 1. Ask your instructor for the codes required before selecting this item.

You are now ready to use the *MicroTools* software.

IBM AND TANDY 1000 START-UP PROCEDURES

FOR *MICROTOOLS: INTEGRATED SOFTWARE FOR WORD PROCESSING, SPREADSHEET, AND DATABASE*

The start-up procedures for the IBM PC, IBM Personal System/2, and Tandy 1000 computers are as follows:

Step 1   Open the door to Disk Drive A and carefully insert your copy of the DOS diskette based on the microcomputer you are using. (If you are using a hard disk drive system do not insert a DOS diskette; instead skip to Step 3.):

   a.   IBM PC - DOS 2.0, 2.1, 3.0, 3.1.

   b.   IBM Personal System/2 - DOS 3.3 or above.

   c.   Tandy 1000 - DOS 2.11

Step 2   Close the door to the disk drive.

Step 3   If the computer is off, turn on all power switches. If the computer is already on, hold down <Ctrl>, <Alt>, and <Del> at the same time. This will boot the system, and the computer will be ready for use.

Step 4   The computer will prompt you to enter the date and time. You may either enter the date (in the MM/DD/YY format) and time (in the HH:MM:SS format), or simply press <Enter> (   ) to bypass these entries. The next line on the screen will then display "A>." (If you are using a hard disk drive system a "C>" will be displayed.)

Step 5 Remove your DOS diskette from Disk Drive A (not necessary if booting from a hard disk in Drive C) and carefully insert your *MicroTools* program diskette. If you are using a hard disk system, enter **A:**.

Step 6 Close the door to the disk drive.

Step 7 Enter **CONTROL**.

Step 8 After a short pause, four screens displaying copyright information will appear. Press <Enter> four times to move through these displays. The Main Menu will appear.

Step 9 Select Change System Features.

Step 10 If the drive specification currently set in Menu Item 1 of the Change System Features menu is the drive that you wish to save your data files to, go to Step 11. If not, enter a **1**. You will be asked to enter the desired drive specification (A, B, or C). If Drive C (hard disk) is keyed, you will be asked to enter a path name or press <Enter>. (Ask your instructor for the path name you are to use.)

Note: If you wish to save data files to your own data diskette, it must first be formatted before it can be used for storage. (For information on formatting a diskette, ask your teacher for assistance.)

Step 11 If the printer type currently set in Menu Item 2 of the Change System Features menu is the type of printer you will be using, go on to Step 12. If not, enter a **2**. Select the desired printer type by keying the appropriate menu choice. Then return to the main menu by pressing <Esc>.

Note: If your printer is not listed, you will need to customize the software for your printer by keying the codes required for bold and underline print modes via Menu Option 1. Ask your instructor for the codes required before selecting this item.

Step 12 Menu Item 3 of the main menu permits you to set the color option to monochrome or color. To change the current setting, enter a **3**, and when the prompt message appears, enter either an **M** for monochrome or a **C** for color.

You are now ready to use the *MicroTools* software.

Appendix A ♦ Start-up Procedures